Hands-On Big Data Analytics with PySpark

Analyze large datasets and discover techniques for testing, immunizing, and parallelizing Spark jobs

Rudy Lai
Bartłomiej Potaczek

BIRMINGHAM - MUMBAI

Hands-On Big Data Analytics with PySpark

Commissioning Editor: Mrinmayee Kawalkar
Acquisition Editor: Joshua Nadar
Content Development Editor: Pratik Andrade
Technical Editor: Sneha Hanchate, Jovita Alva, Snehal Dalmet
Copy Editor: Safis Editing
Project Coordinator: Namrata Swetta
Proofreader: Safis Editing
Indexer: Tejal Daruwale Soni
Graphics: Jisha Chirayil
Production Coordinator: Shraddha Falebhai

First published: March 2019

Production reference: 1280319

Published by Packt Publishing Ltd.
Livery Place
35 Livery Street
Birmingham
B3 2PB, UK.

ISBN 978-1-83864-413-0

www.packtpub.com

`mapt.io`

Mapt is an online digital library that gives you full access to over 5,000 books and videos, as well as industry-leading tools to help you plan your personal development and advance your career. For more information, please visit our website.

Why subscribe?

- Spend less time learning and more time coding with practical eBooks and Videos from over 4,000 industry professionals

- Improve your learning with Skill Plans built especially for you

- Get a free eBook or video every month

- Mapt is fully searchable

- Copy and paste, print, and bookmark content

Packt.com

Did you know that Packt offers eBook versions of every book published, with PDF and ePub files available? You can upgrade to the eBook version at `www.packt.com` and as a print book customer, you are entitled to a discount on the eBook copy. Get in touch with us at `customercare@packtpub.com` for more details.

At `www.packt.com`, you can also read a collection of free technical articles, sign up for a range of free newsletters, and receive exclusive discounts and offers on Packt books and eBooks.

Contributors

About the authors

Colibri Digital is a technology consultancy company founded in 2015 by James Cross and Ingrid Funie. The company works to help its clients navigate the rapidly changing and complex world of emerging technologies, with deep expertise in areas such as big data, data science, machine learning, and cloud computing. Over the past few years, they have worked with some of the world's largest and most prestigious companies, including a tier 1 investment bank, a leading management consultancy group, and one of the world's most popular soft drinks companies, helping each of them to better make sense of their data, and process it in more intelligent ways. The company lives by its motto: Data -> Intelligence -> Action.

Rudy Lai is the founder of QuantCopy, a sales acceleration start-up using AI to write sales emails to prospective customers. Prior to founding QuantCopy, Rudy ran HighDimension.IO, a machine learning consultancy, where he experienced first hand the frustrations of outbound sales and prospecting. Rudy has also spent more than 5 years in quantitative trading at leading investment banks such as Morgan Stanley. This valuable experience allowed him to witness the power of data, but also the pitfalls of automation using data science and machine learning. He holds a computer science degree from Imperial College London, where he was part of the Dean's list, and received awards including the Deutsche Bank Artificial Intelligence prize.

Bartłomiej Potaczek is a software engineer working for Schibsted Tech Polska and programming mostly in JavaScript. He is a big fan of everything related to the react world, functional programming, and data visualization. He founded and created InitLearn, a portal that allows users to learn to program in a pair-programming fashion. He was also involved in InitLearn frontend, which is built on the React-Redux technologies. Besides programming, he enjoys football and crossfit. Currently, he is working on rewriting the frontend for tv.nu—Sweden's most complete TV guide, with over 200 channels. He has also recently worked on technologies including React, React Router, and Redux.

Packt is searching for authors like you

If you're interested in becoming an author for Packt, please visit authors.packtpub.com and apply today. We have worked with thousands of developers and tech professionals, just like you, to help them share their insight with the global tech community. You can make a general application, apply for a specific hot topic that we are recruiting an author for, or submit your own idea.

Table of Contents

Preface

Apache Spark is an open source, parallel processing framework that has been around for quite some time now. One of the many uses of Apache Spark is for data analytics applications across clustered computers.

This book will help you implement some practical and proven techniques to improve aspects of programming and administration in Apache Spark. You will not only learn how to use Spark and the Python API to create high-performance analytics with big data, but also discover techniques to test, immunize, and parallelize Spark jobs.

This book covers the installation and setup of PySpark, RDD operations, big data cleaning and wrangling, and aggregating and summarizing data into useful reports. You will learn how to source data from all popular data hosting platforms, including HDFS, Hive, JSON, and S3, and deal with large datasets with PySpark to gain practical big data experience. This book will also help you to work on prototypes on local machines and subsequently go on to handle messy data in production and on a large scale.

Who this book is for

This book is for developers, data scientists, business analysts, or anyone who needs to reliably analyze large amounts of large-scale, real-world data. Whether you're tasked with creating your company's business intelligence function, or creating great data platforms for your machine learning models, or looking to use code to magnify the impact of your business, this book is for you.

What this book covers

Chapter 1, *Installing Pyspark and Setting up Your Development Environment*, covers the installation of PySpark and learning about core concepts in Spark, including **resilient distributed datasets (RDDs)**, SparkContext, and Spark tools, such as SparkConf and SparkShell.

Chapter 2, *Getting Your Big Data into the Spark Environment Using RDDs*, explains how to get your big data into the Spark environment using RDDs using a wide array of tools to interact and modify this data so that useful insights can be extracted.

Chapter 3, *Big Data Cleaning and Wrangling with Spark Notebooks*, covers how to use Spark in notebook applications, thereby facilitating the effective use of RDDs.

Chapter 4, *Aggregating and Summarizing Data into Useful Reports*, describes how to calculate averages with the map and reduce function, perform faster average computation, and use a pivot table with key/value pair data points.

Chapter 5, *Powerful Exploratory Data Analysis with MLlib*, examines Spark's ability to perform regression tasks with models including linear regression and SVMs.

Chapter 6, *Putting Structure on Your Big Data with SparkSQL*, explains how to manipulate DataFrames with Spark SQL schemas, and use the Spark DSL to build queries for structured data operations.

Chapter 7, *Transformations and Actions*, looks at Spark transformations to defer computations and then considers transformations that should be avoided. We will also use the `reduce` and `reduceByKey` methods to carry out calculations from a dataset.

Chapter 8, *Immutable Design*, explains how to use DataFrame operations for transformations with a view to discussing immutability in a highly concurrent environment.

Chapter 9, *Avoid Shuffle and Reduce Operational Expenses*, covers shuffling and the operations of Spark API that should be used. We will then test operations that cause a shuffle in Apache Spark to know which operations should be avoided.

Chapter 10, *Saving Data in the Correct Format*, explains how to save data in the correct format and also save data in plain text using Spark's standard API.

Chapter 11, *Working with the Spark Key/Value API*, discusses the transformations available on key/value pairs. We will look at actions on key/value pairs and look at the available partitioners on key/value data.

Chapter 12, *Testing Apache Spark Jobs*, goes into further detail about testing Apache Spark jobs in different versions of Spark.

Chapter 13, *Leveraging the Spark GraphX API*, covers how to leverage Spark GraphX API. We will carry out experiments with the Edge API and Vertex API.

To get the most out of this book

This book requires some basic programming experience in PySpark, Python, Java, and Scala.

Download the example code files

You can download the example code files for this book from your account at `www.packt.com`. If you purchased this book elsewhere, you can visit `www.packt.com/support` and register to have the files emailed directly to you.

You can download the code files by following these steps:

1. Log in or register at `www.packt.com`.
2. Select the **SUPPORT** tab.
3. Click on **Code Downloads & Errata**.
4. Enter the name of the book in the **Search** box and follow the onscreen instructions.

Once the file is downloaded, please make sure that you unzip or extract the folder using the latest version of:

- WinRAR/7-Zip for Windows
- Zipeg/iZip/UnRarX for Mac
- 7-Zip/PeaZip for Linux

The code bundle for the book is also hosted on GitHub at `https://github.com/PacktPublishing/Hands-On-Big-Data-Analytics-with-PySpark`. In case there's an update to the code, it will be updated on the existing GitHub repository.

We also have other code bundles from our rich catalog of books and videos available at `https://github.com/PacktPublishing/`. Check them out!

Download the color images

We also provide a PDF file that has color images of the screenshots/diagrams used in this book. You can download it here: `http://www.packtpub.com/sites/default/files/downloads/9781838644130_ColorImages.pdf`.

Conventions used

There are a number of text conventions used throughout this book.

`CodeInText`: Indicates code words in text, database table names, folder names, filenames, file extensions, pathnames, dummy URLs, user input, and Twitter handles. Here is an example: "Mount the downloaded `WebStorm-10*.dmg` disk image file as another disk in your system."

A block of code is set as follows:

```
test("Should use immutable DF API") {
    import spark.sqlContext.implicits._
    //given
    val userData =
        spark.sparkContext.makeRDD(List(
            UserData("a", "1"),
            UserData("b", "2"),
            UserData("d", "200")
        )).toDF()
```

When we wish to draw your attention to a particular part of a code block, the relevant lines or items are set in bold:

```
class ImmutableRDD extends FunSuite {
    val spark: SparkContext = SparkSession
        .builder().master("local[2]").getOrCreate().sparkContext

test("RDD should be immutable") {
    //given
    val data = spark.makeRDD(0 to 5)
```

Any command-line input or output is written as follows:

```
total_duration/(normal_data.count())
```

Bold: Indicates a new term, an important word, or words that you see on screen. For example, words in menus or dialog boxes appear in the text like this. Here is an example: "Select **System info** from the **Administration** panel."

Warnings or important notes appear like this.

 Tips and tricks appear like this.

Get in touch

Feedback from our readers is always welcome.

General feedback: If you have questions about any aspect of this book, mention the book title in the subject of your message and email us at customercare@packtpub.com.

Errata: Although we have taken every care to ensure the accuracy of our content, mistakes do happen. If you have found a mistake in this book, we would be grateful if you would report this to us. Please visit www.packt.com/submit-errata, selecting your book, clicking on the Errata Submission Form link, and entering the details.

Piracy: If you come across any illegal copies of our works in any form on the internet, we would be grateful if you would provide us with the location address or website name. Please contact us at copyright@packt.com with a link to the material.

If you are interested in becoming an author: If there is a topic that you have expertise in, and you are interested in either writing or contributing to a book, please visit authors.packtpub.com.

Reviews

Please leave a review. Once you have read and used this book, why not leave a review on the site that you purchased it from? Potential readers can then see and use your unbiased opinion to make purchase decisions, we at Packt can understand what you think about our products, and our authors can see your feedback on their book. Thank you!

For more information about Packt, please visit packt.com.

1
Installing Pyspark and Setting up Your Development Environment

In this chapter, we are going to introduce Spark and learn the core concepts, such as, SparkContext, and Spark tools such as SparkConf and Spark shell. The only prerequisite is the knowledge of basic Python concepts and the desire to seek insight from big data. We will learn how to analyze and discover patterns with Spark SQL to improve our business intelligence. Also, you will be able to quickly iterate through your solution by setting to PySpark for your own computer. By the end of the book, you will be able to work with real-life messy data sets using PySpark to get practical big data experience.

In this chapter, we will cover the following topics:

- An overview of PySpark
- Setting up Spark on Windows and PySpark
- Core concepts in Spark and PySpark

An overview of PySpark

Before we start with installing PySpark, which is the Python interface for Spark, let's go through some core concepts in Spark and PySpark. Spark is the latest big data tool from Apache, which can be found by simply going to `http://spark.apache.org/`. It's a unified analytics engine for large-scale data processing. This means that, if you have a lot of data, you can feed that data into Spark to create some analytics at a good speed. If we look at the running times between Hadoop and Spark, Spark is more than a hundred times faster than Hadoop. It is very easy to use because there are very good APIs for use with Spark.

The four major components of the Spark platform are as follows:

- **Spark SQL**: A clearing language for Spark
- **Spark Streaming**: Allows you to feed in real-time streaming data
- **MLlib (machine learning)**: The machine learning library for Spark
- **GraphX (graph)**: The graphing library for Spark

The core concept in Spark is an RDD, which is similar to the pandas DataFrame, or a Python dictionary or list. It is a way for Spark to store large amounts of data on the infrastructure for us. The key difference of an RDD versus something that is in your local memory, such as a pandas DataFrame, is that an RDD is distributed across many machines, but it appears like one unified dataset. What this means is, if you have large amounts of data that you want to operate on in parallel, you can put it in an RDD and Spark will handle parallelization and the clustering of the data for you.

Spark has three different interfaces, as follows:

- Scala
- Java
- Python

Python is similar to PySpark integration, which we will cover soon. For now, we will import some libraries from the PySpark package to help us work with Spark. The best way for us to understand Spark is to look at an example, as shown in the following screenshot:

```
lines = sc.textFile("data.txt")
lineLengths = lines.map(lambda s: len(s))
totalLength = lineLengths.reduce(lambda a, b: a + b)
```

In the preceding code, we have created a new variable called `lines` by calling `SC.textFile ("data.txt")`. `sc` is our Python objects that represent our Spark cluster. A Spark cluster is a series of instances or cloud computers that store our Spark processes. By calling a `textFile` constructor and feeding in `data.text`, we have potentially fed in a large text file and created an RDD just using this one line. In other words, what we are trying to do here is to feed a large text file into a distributed cluster and Spark, and Spark handles this clustering for us.

In line two and line three, we have a MapReduce function. In line two, we have mapped the length function using a `lambda` function to each line of `data.text`. In line three, we have called a reduction function to add all `lineLengths` together to produce the total length of the documents. While Python's `lines` is a variable that contains all the lines in `data.text`, under the hood, Spark is actually handling the distribution of fragments of `data.text` in two different instances on the Spark cluster, and is handling the MapReduce computation over all of these instances.

Spark SQL

Spark SQL is one of the four components on top of the Spark platform, as we saw earlier in the chapter. It can be used to execute SQL queries or read data from any existing Hive insulation, where Hive is a database implementation also from Apache. Spark SQL looks very similar to MySQL or Postgres. The following code snippet is a good example:

```
#Register the DataFrame as a SQL temporary view
df.CreateOrReplaceTempView("people")

sqlDF = spark.sql("SELECT * FROM people")
sqlDF.show()

#+----+-------+
#| age|   name|
#+----+-------+
#+null|Jackson|
#|  30| Martin|
#|  19| Melvin|
#+----|-------|
```

You'll need to select all the columns from a certain table, such as `people`, and using the Spark objects, you'll feed in a very standard-looking SQL statement, which is going to show an SQL result much like what you would expect from a normal SQL implementation.

Let's now look at datasets and DataFrames. A dataset is a distributed collection of data. It is an interface added in Spark 1.6 that provides benefits on top of RDDs. A DataFrame, on the other hand, is very familiar to those who have used pandas or R. A DataFrame is simply a dataset organized into named columns, which is similar to a relational database or a DataFrame in Python. The main difference between a dataset and a DataFrame is that DataFrames have column names. As you can imagine, this would be very convenient for machine learning work and feeding into things such as scikit-learn.

Let's look at how DataFrames can be used. The following code snippet is a quick example of a DataFrame:

```
# spark is an existing SparkSession
df = spark.read.json("examples/src/main/resources/people.json")
# Displays the content of the DataFrame to stdout
df.show()

#+----+-------+
#| age|   name|
#+----+-------+
#+null|Jackson|
#|  30| Martin|
#|  19| Melvin|
#+----|-------|
```

In the same way, as pandas or R would do, `read.json` allows us to feed in some data from a JSON file, and `df.show` shows us the contents of the DataFrame in a similar way to pandas.

MLlib, as we know, is used to make machine learning scalable and easy. MLlib allows you to do common machine learning tasks, such as featurization; creating pipelines; saving and loading algorithms, models, and pipelines; and also some utilities, such as linear algebra, statistics, and data handling. The other thing to note is that Spark and RDD are almost inseparable concepts. If your main use case for Spark is machine learning, Spark now actually encourages you to use the DataFrame-based API for MLlib, which is quite beneficial to us as we are already familiar with pandas, which means a smooth transition into Spark.

In the next section, we will see how we can set up Spark on Windows, and set up PySpark as the interface.

Setting up Spark on Windows and PySpark

Complete the following steps to install PySpark on a Windows machine:

1. Download **Gnu on Windows (GOW)** from `https://github.com/bmatzelle/gow/releases/download/v0.8.0/Gow-0.8.0.exe`.
2. GOW allows the use of Linux commands on Windows. We can use the following command to see the basic Linux commands allowed by installing GOW:

    ```
    gow --list
    ```

This gives the following output:

```
C:\Users\Admin>gow --list
Available executables:

awk, basename, bash, bc, bison, bunzip2, bzip2, bzip2recover, cat,
chgrp, chmod, chown, chroot, cksum, clear, cp, csplit, curl, cut, dc,
dd, df, diff, diff3, dirname, dos2unix, du, egrep, env, expand, expr,
factor, fgrep, flex, fmt, fold, gawk, gfind, gow, grep, gsar, gsort,
gzip, head, hostid, hostname, id, indent, install, join, jwhois, less,
lesskey, ln, ls, m4, make, md5sum, mkdir, mkfifo, mknod, mv, nano,
ncftp, nl, od, pageant, paste, patch, pathchk, plink, pr, printenv,
printf, pscp, psftp, putty, puttygen, pwd, rm, rmdir, scp, sdiff, sed,
seq, sftp, sha1sum, shar, sleep, split, ssh, su, sum, sync, tac, tail,
tar, tee, test, touch, tr, uname, unexpand, uniq, unix2dos, unlink,
unrar, unshar, uudecode, uuencode, vim, wc, wget, whereis, which,
whoami, xargs, yes, zip

C:\Users\Admin>
```

3. Download and install Anaconda. If you need help, you can go through the following tutorial: `https://medium.com/@GalarnykMichael/install-python-on-windows-anaconda-c63c7c3d1444`.
4. Close the previous command line and open a new command line.
5. Go to the Apache Spark website (`https://spark.apache.org/`).
6. To download Spark, choose the following from the drop-down menu:
   - A recent Spark release
   - A proper package type

The following screenshot shows the download page of Apache Spark:

Download Apache Spark™

1. Choose a Spark release: `2.3.3 (Feb 15 2019) ▼`

2. Choose a package type: `Pre-built for Apache Hadoop 2.7 and later        ▼`

3. Download Spark: spark-2.3.3-bin-hadoop2.7.tgz

4. Verify this release using the 2.3.3 signatures, checksums and project release KEYS.

7. Then, download Spark. Once it is downloaded, move the file to the folder where you want to unzip it.
8. You can either unzip it manually or use the following commands:

```
gzip -d spark-2.1.0-bin-hadoop2.7.tgz
tar xvf spark-2.1.0-bin-hadoop2.7.tar
```

9. Now, download `winutils.exe` into your `spark-2.1.0-bin-hadoop2.7\bin` folder using the following command:

   ```
   curl -k -L -o winutils.exe
   https://github.com/steveloughran/winutils/blob/master/hadoop-2.6.0/
   bin/winutils.exe?raw=true
   ```

10. Make sure you have Java installed on your machine. You can use the following command to see the Java version:

    ```
    java --version
    ```

    This gives the following output:

    ```
    C:\>java -version
    java version "1.8.0_201"
    Java(TM) SE Runtime Environment (build 1.8.0_201-b09)
    Java HotSpot(TM) Client VM (build 25.201-b09, mixed mode, sharing)

    C:\>
    ```

11. Check for the Python version by using the following command:

    ```
    python --version
    ```

    This gives the following output:

    ```
    C:\>python --version
    Python 3.7.0
    ```

12. Let's edit our environmental variables so that we can open Spark in any directory, as follows:

    ```
    setx SPARK_HOME C:\opt\spark\spark-2.1.0-bin-hadoop2.7
    setx HADOOP_HOME C:\opt\spark\spark-2.1.0-bin-hadoop2.7
    setx PYSPARK_DRIVER_PYTHON ipython
    setx PYSPARK_DRIVER_PYTHON_OPTS notebook
    ```

    Add `C:\opt\spark\spark-2.1.0-bin-hadoop2.7\bin` to your path.

13. Close the Terminal, open a new one, and type the following command:

    ```
    --master local[2]
    ```

The `PYSPARK_DRIVER_PYTHON` and the `PYSPARK_DRIVER_PYTHON_OPTS` parameters are used to launch the PySpark shell in Jupyter Notebook. The `--master` parameter is used for setting the master node address.

14. The next thing to do is to run the PySpark command in the `bin` folder:

   `.\bin\pyspark`

   This gives the following output:

```
c:\opt\spark\spark-2.1.0-bin-hadoop2.7>.\bin\pyspark
[TerminalIPythonApp] WARNING | Subcommand `ipython notebook` is deprecated and will be removed in future versions.
[TerminalIPythonApp] WARNING | You likely want to use `jupyter notebook` in the future
[I 18:58:16.992 NotebookApp] [nb_conda_kernels] enabled, 0 kernels found
[I 18:58:17.060 NotebookApp] JupyterLab extension loaded from C:\Users\Admin\Anaconda3\lib\site-packages\jupyterlab
[I 18:58:17.060 NotebookApp] JupyterLab application directory is C:\Users\Admin\Anaconda3\share\jupyter\lab
[I 18:58:17.409 NotebookApp] [nb_conda] enabled
[I 18:58:17.410 NotebookApp] Serving notebooks from local directory: c:\opt\spark\spark-2.1.0-bin-hadoop2.7
[I 18:58:17.415 NotebookApp] The Jupyter Notebook is running at:
[I 18:58:17.415 NotebookApp] http://localhost:8888/?token=9d6838b0bacad0c6083861cf7378a1379719f1ccc22879a7
[I 18:58:17.416 NotebookApp] Use Control-C to stop this server and shut down all kernels (twice to skip confirmation).
[C 18:58:17.476 NotebookApp]

    Copy/paste this URL into your browser when you connect for the first time,
    to login with a token:
        http://localhost:8888/?token=9d6838b0bacad0c6083861cf7378a1379719f1ccc22879a7
[I 18:58:17.767 NotebookApp] Accepting one-time-token-authenticated connection from ::1
```

Core concepts in Spark and PySpark

Let's now look at the following core concepts in Spark and PySpark:

- SparkContext
- SparkConf
- Spark shell

SparkContext

SparkContext is an object or concept within Spark. It is a big data analytical engine that allows you to programmatically harness the power of Spark.

The power of Spark can be seen when you have a large amount of data that doesn't fit into your local machine or your laptop, so you need two or more computers to process it. You also need to maintain the speed of processing this data while working on it. We not only want the data to be split among a few computers for computation; we also want the computation to be parallel. Lastly, you want this computation to look like one single computation.

Let's consider an example where we have a large contact database that has 50 million names, and we might want to extract the first name from each of these contacts. Obviously, it is difficult to fit 50 million names into your local memory, especially if each name is embedded within a larger contacts object. This is where Spark comes into the picture. Spark allows you to give it a big data file, and will help in handling and uploading this data file, while handling all the operations carried out on this data for you. This power is managed by Spark's cluster manager, as shown in the following diagram:

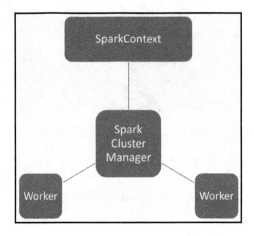

The cluster manager manages multiple workers; there could be 2, 3, or even 100. The main point is that Spark's technology helps in managing this cluster of workers, and you need a way to control how the cluster is behaving, and also pass data back and forth from the clustered rate.

A **SparkContext** lets you use the power of Spark's cluster manager as with Python objects. So with a **SparkContext**, you can pass jobs and resources, schedule tasks, and complete tasks the downstream from the **SparkContext** down to the **Spark Cluster Manager**, which will then take the results back from the **Spark Cluster Manager** once it has completed its computation.

Let's see what this looks like in practice and see how to set up a SparkContext:

1. First, we need to import `SparkContext`.
2. Create a new object in the `sc` variable standing for the SparkContext using the `SparkContext` constructor.
3. In the `SparkContext` constructor, pass a `local` context. We are looking at `hands on PySpark` in this context, as follows:

```
from pyspark import SparkContext
sc = SparkContext('local', 'hands on PySpark')
```

4. After we've established this, all we need to do is then use `sc` as an entry point to our Spark operation, as demonstrated in the following code snippet:

```
visitors = [10, 3, 35, 25, 41, 9, 29]
df_visitors = sc.parallelize(visitors)
df_visitors_yearly = df_visitors.map(lambda x: x*365).collect()
print(df_visitors_yearly)
```

Let's take an example; if we were to analyze the synthetic datasets of visitor counts to our clothing store, we might have a list of `visitors` denoting the daily visitors to our store. We can then create a parallelized version of the DataFrame, call `sc.parallelize(visitors)`, and feed in the `visitors` datasets. `df_visitors` then creates for us a DataFrame of visitors. We can then map a function; for example, making the daily numbers and extrapolating them into a yearly number by mapping a `lambda` function that multiplies the daily number (x) by `365`, which is the number of days in a year. Then, we call a `collect()` function to make sure that Spark executes on this `lambda` call. Lastly, we print out `df_ visitors_yearly`. Now, we have Spark working on this computation on our synthetic data behind the scenes, while this is simply a Python operation.

Spark shell

We will go back into our Spark folder, which is `spark-2.3.2-bin-hadoop2.7`, and start our PySpark binary by typing `.\bin\pyspark`.

We can see that we've started a shell session with Spark in the following screenshot:

```
10-26 13:27:44 spark-2.3.2-bin-hadoop2.7
> .\bin\pyspark
Python 3.6.2 (v3.6.2:5fd33b5, Jul  8 2017, 04:57:36) [MSC v.1900 64 bit (AMD64)] on win32
Type "help", "copyright", "credits" or "license" for more information.
WARNING: An illegal reflective access operation has occurred
WARNING: Illegal reflective access by org.apache.hadoop.security.authentication.util.KerberosUtil (f
ile:/C:/spark/spark-2.3.2-bin-hadoop2.7/spark-2.3.2-bin-hadoop2.7/jars/hadoop-auth-2.7.3.jar) to met
hod sun.security.krb5.Config.getInstance()
WARNING: Please consider reporting this to the maintainers of org.apache.hadoop.security.authenticat
ion.util.KerberosUtil
WARNING: Use --illegal-access=warn to enable warnings of further illegal reflective access operation
s
WARNING: All illegal access operations will be denied in a future release
2018-10-26 13:28:15 WARN  NativeCodeLoader:62 - Unable to load native-hadoop library for your platfo
rm... using builtin-java classes where applicable
Setting default log level to "WARN".
To adjust logging level use sc.setLogLevel(newLevel). For SparkR, use setLogLevel(newLevel).
Welcome to
      ____              __
     / __/__  ___ _____/ /__
    _\ \/ _ \/ _ `/ __/  '_/
   /__ / .__/\_,_/_/ /_/\_\   version 2.3.2
      /_/

Using Python version 3.6.2 (v3.6.2:5fd33b5, Jul  8 2017 04:57:36)
SparkSession available as 'spark'.
>>>
```

Spark is now available to us as a `spark` variable. Let's try a simple thing in Spark. The first thing to do is to load a random file. In each Spark installation, there is a `README.md` markdown file, so let's load it into our memory as follows:

```
text_file = spark.read.text("README.md")
```

If we use `spark.read.text` and then put in `README.md`, we get a few warnings, but we shouldn't be too concerned about that at the moment, as we will see later how we are going to fix these things. The main thing here is that we can use Python syntax to access Spark.

What we have done here is put `README.md` as text data read by `spark` into Spark, and we can use `text_file.count()` can get Spark to count how many characters are in our text file as follows:

```
text_file.count()
```

From this, we get the following output:

```
103
```

We can also see what the first line is with the following:

```
text_file.first()
```

We will get the following output:

```
Row(value='# Apache Spark')
```

We can now count a number of lines that contain the word Spark by doing the following:

```
lines_with_spark = text_file.filter(text_file.value.contains("Spark"))
```

Here, we have filtered for lines using the filter() function, and within the filter() function, we have specified that text_file_value.contains includes the word "Spark", and we have put those results into the lines_with_spark variable.

We can modify the preceding command and simply add .count(), as follows:

```
text_file.filter(text_file.value.contains("Spark")).count()
```

We will now get the following output:

```
20
```

We can see that 20 lines in the text file contain the word Spark. This is just a simple example of how we can use the Spark shell.

SparkConf

SparkConf allows us to configure a Spark application. It sets various Spark parameters as key-value pairs, and so will usually create a SparkConf object with a SparkConf() constructor, which would then load values from the spark.* underlying Java system.

There are a few useful functions; for example, we can use the sets() function to set the configuration property. We can use the setMaster() function to set the master URL to connect to. We can use the setAppName() function to set the application name, and setSparkHome() in order to set the path where Spark will be installed on worker nodes.

 You can learn more about SparkConf at https://spark.apache.org/ docs/0.9.0/api/pyspark/pysaprk.conf.SparkConf-class.html.

Summary

In this chapter, we learned about the core concepts in Spark and PySpark. We learned about setting up Spark and using PySpark on Windows. We also went through the three main pillars of Spark, which are SparkContext, Spark shell, and SparkConf.

In the next chapter, we're going to look at getting your big data into Spark environments using RDDs.

2
Getting Your Big Data into the Spark Environment Using RDDs

Primarily, this chapter will provide a brief overview of how to get your big data into the Spark environment using **resilient distributed datasets** (**RDDs**). We will be using a wide array of tools to interact with and modify this data so that useful insights can be extracted. We will first load the data on Spark RDDs and then carry out parallelization with Spark RDDs.

In this chapter, we will cover the following topics:

- Loading data onto Spark RDDs
- Parallelization with Spark RDDs
- Basics of RDD operation

Loading data on to Spark RDDs

In this section, we are going to look at loading data on to Spark RDDs, and will cover the following topics:

- The UCI machine learning data repository
- Getting data from the repository to Python
- Getting data into Spark

Let's start with an overview of the UCI machine learning data repository.

The UCI machine learning repository

We can access the UCI machine learning repository by navigating to `https://archive.ics.uci.edu/ml/`. So, what is the UCI machine learning repository? UCI stands for the University of California Irvine machine learning repository, and it is a very useful resource for getting open source and free datasets for machine learning. Although PySpark's main issue or solution doesn't concern machine learning, we can use this as a chance to get big datasets that help us test out the functions of PySpark.

Let's take a look at the KDD Cup 1999 dataset, which we will download, and then we will load the whole dataset into PySpark.

Getting the data from the repository to Spark

We can follow these steps to download the dataset and load it in PySpark:

1. Click on **Data Folder**.
2. You will be redirected to a folder that has various files as follows:

Index of /ml/machine-learning-databases/kddcup99-mld

Name	Last modified	Size	Description
Parent Directory		-	
corrected.gz	16-May-2000 08:50	1.3M	
kddcup.data.gz	26-Jun-2007 12:59	17M	
kddcup.data_10_percent.gz	26-Jun-2007 12:59	2.0M	
kddcup.names	23-Oct-2012 11:03	1.3K	
kddcup.newtestdata_10_percent_unlabeled.gz	28-Oct-1999 11:23	1.3M	
kddcup.testdata.unlabeled.gz	28-Oct-1999 11:23	11M	
kddcup.testdata.unlabeled_10_percent.gz	28-Oct-1999 11:23	1.3M	
kddcup99.html	23-Oct-2012 11:03	2.4K	
task.html	23-Oct-2012 11:03	10K	
training_attack_types	23-Oct-2012 11:03	272	
typo-correction.txt	23-Oct-2012 11:03	825	

Apache/2.2.15 (CentOS) Server at archive.ics.uci.edu Port 443

You can see that there's **kddcup.data.gz**, and there is also 10% of that data available in **kddcup.data_10_percent.gz**. We will be working with food datasets. To work with the food datasets, right-click on **kddcup.data.gz**, select **Copy link address**, and then go back to the PySpark console and import the data.

Let's take a look at how this works using the following steps:

1. After launching PySpark, the first thing we need to do is import `urllib`, which is a library that allows us to interact with resources on the internet, as follows:

```
import urllib.request
```

2. The next thing to do is use this `request` library to pull some resources from the internet, as shown in the following code:

```
f =
urllib.request.urlretrieve("https://archive.ics.uci.edu/ml/machine-
learning-databases/kddcup99-mld/kddcup.data.gz"),"kddcup.data.gz"
```

This command will take some time to process. Once the file has been downloaded, we can see that Python has returned and the console is active.

3. Next, load this using `SparkContext`. So, `SparkContext` is materialized or objectified in Python as the `sc` variable, as follows:

```
sc
```

This output is as demonstrated in the following code snippet:

```
SparkContext
Spark UI
Version
 v2.3.3
Master
 local[*]
AppName
 PySparkShell
```

Getting data into Spark

1. Next, load the KDD cup data into PySpark using `sc`, as shown in the following command:

```
raw_data = sc.textFile("./kddcup.data.gz")
```

2. In the following command, we can see that the raw data is now in the `raw_data` variable:

    ```
    raw_data
    ```

    This output is as demonstrated in the following code snippet:

    ```
    ./kddcup.data,gz MapPartitionsRDD[3] at textFile at
    NativeMethodAccessorImpl.java:0
    ```

If we enter the `raw_data` variable, it gives us details regarding `kddcup.data.gz`, where raw data underlying the data file is located, and tells us about `MapPartitionsRDD`.

Now that we know how to load the data into Spark, let's learn about parallelization with Spark RDDs.

Parallelization with Spark RDDs

Now that we know how to create RDDs within the text file that we received from the internet, we can look at a different way to create this RDD. Let's discuss parallelization with our Spark RDDs.

In this section, we will cover the following topics:

- What is parallelization?
- How do we parallelize Spark RDDs?

Let's start with parallelization.

What is parallelization?

The best way to understand Spark, or any language, is to look at the documentation. If we look at Spark's documentation, it clearly states that, for the `textFile` function that we used last time, it reads the text file from HDFS.

On the other hand, if we look at the definition of `parallelize`, we can see that this is creating an RDD by distributing a local Scala collection.

So, the main difference between using `parallelize` to create an RDD and using the `textFile` to create an RDD is where the data is sourced from.

Let's look at how this works practically. Let's go to the PySpark installation screen, from where we left off previously. So, we imported `urllib`, we used `urllib.request` to retrieve some data from the internet, and we used `SparkContext` and `textFile` to load this data into Spark. The other way to do this is to use `parallelize`.

Let's look at how we can do this. Let's first assume that our data is already in Python, and so, for demonstration purposes, we are going to create a Python list of a hundred numbers as follows:

```
a = range(100)
a
```

This gives us the following output:

```
range(0, 100)
```

For example, if we look at `a`, it is simply a list of 100 numbers. If we convert this into a `list`, it will show us the list of 100 numbers:

```
list (a)
```

This gives us the following output:

```
[0,
 1,
 2,
 3,
 4,
 5,
 6,
 7,
 8,
 9,
 10,
 11,
 12,
 13,
 14,
 15,
 16,
 17,
 18,
 19,
 20,
```

```
21,
22,
23,
24,
25,
26,
27,
...
```

The following command shows us how to turn this into an RDD:

```
list_rdd = sc.parallelize(a)
```

If we look at what `list_rdd` contains, we can see that it is `PythonRDD.scala:52`, so, this tells us that the Scala-backed PySpark instance has recognized this as a Python-created RDD, as follows:

```
list_rdd
```

This gives us the following output:

```
PythonRDD[3] at RDD at PythonRDD.scala:52
```

Now, let's look at what we can do with this list. The first thing we can do is count how many elements are present in `list_rdd` by using the following command:

```
list_rdd.count()
```

This gives us the following output:

```
100
```

We can see that `list_rdd` is counted at 100. If we run it again without cutting through into the results, we can actually see that, since Scala is running in a real time when going through the RDD, it is slower than just running the length of `a`, which is instant.

However, RDD takes some time, because it needs time to go through the parallelized version of the list. So, at small scales, where there are only a hundred numbers, it might not be very helpful to have this trade-off, but with larger amounts of data and larger individual sizes of the elements of the data, it will make a lot more sense.

We can also take an arbitrary amount of elements from the list, as follows:

```
list_rdd.take(10)
```

This gives us the following output:

```
[0, 1, 2, 3, 4, 5, 6, 7, 8, 9]
```

When we run the preceding command, we can see that PySpark has performed some calculations before returning the first ten elements of the list. Notice that all of this is now backed by PySpark, and we are using Spark's power to manipulate this list of 100 items.

Let's now use the reduce function in `list_rdd`, or in RDDs in general, to demonstrate what we can do with PySpark's RDDs. We will apply two parameter functions as an anonymous `lambda` function to the `reduce` call as follows:

```
list_rdd.reduce(lambda a, b: a+b)
```

Here, `lambda` takes two parameters, `a` and `b`. It simply adds these two numbers together, hence a+b, and returns the output. With the RDD `reduce` call, we can sequentially add the first two numbers of RDD lists together, return the results, and then add the third number to the results, and so on. So, eventually, you add all 100 numbers to the same results by using `reduce`.

Now, after some work through the distributed database, we can now see that adding numbers from 0 to 99 gives us 4950, and it is all done using PySpark's RDD methodology. You might recognize this function from the term MapReduce, and, indeed, it's the same thing.

We have just learned what parallelization is in PySpark, and how we can parallelize Spark RDDs. This effectively amounts to another way for us to create RDDs, and that's very useful for us. Now, let's look at some basics of RDD operation.

Basics of RDD operation

Let's now go through some RDD operational basics. The best way to understand what something does is to look at the documentation so that we can get a rigorous understanding of what a function performs.

The reason why this is very important is that the documentation is the golden source of how a function is defined and what it is designed to be used as. By reading the documentation, we make sure that we are as close to the source as possible in our understanding. The link to the relevant documentation is `https://spark.apache.org/docs/latest/rdd-programming-guide.html`.

So, let's start with the map function. The map function returns an RDD by applying the f function to each element of this RDD. In other words, it works the same as the map function we see in Python. On the other hand, the filter function returns a new RDD containing only the elements that satisfy a predicate, and that predicate, which is a Boolean, is often returned by an f function fed into the filter function. Again, this works very similarly to the filter function in Python. Lastly, the collect() function returns a list that contains all the elements in this RDD. And this is where I think reading the documentation really shines, when we see notes like this. This would never come up in Stack Overflow or a blog post if you were simply googling what this is.

So, we're saying that collect() should only be used if the resulting array is expected to be small, as all the data is loaded in a driver's memory. What that means is, if we think back on Chapter 01, *Installing PySpark and Setting Up Your Development Environment*, Spark is superb because it can collect and parallelize data across many different unique machines, and have it transparently operatable from one Terminal. What collects notes is saying is that, if we call collect(), the resulting RDD would be completely loaded into the driver's memory, in which case we lose the benefits of distributing the data around a cluster of Spark instances.

Now that we know all of this, let's see how we actually apply these three functions to our data. So, go back to the PySpark Terminal; we have already loaded our raw data as a text file, as we have seen in previous chapters.

We will write a filter function to find all the lines to indicate RDD data, where each line contains the word normal, as seen in the following screenshot:

```
contains_normal = raw_data.filter(lambda line: "normal." in line)
```

Let's analyze what this means. Firstly, we are calling the filter function for the RDD raw data, and we're feeding it an anonymous lambda function that takes one line parameter and returns the predicates, as we have read in the documentation, on whether or not the word normal exists in the line. At this moment, as we have discussed in the previous chapters, we haven't actually computed this filter operation. What we need to do is call a function that actually consolidates the data and forces Spark to calculate something. In this case, we can count on contains_normal, as demonstrated in the following screenshot:

```
>>> contains_normal.count()
972781
>>>
```

You can see that it has counted just over 970,000 lines in the raw data that contain the word normal. To use the filter function, we provide it with the lambda function and use a consolidating function, such as counts, that forces Spark to calculate and compute the data in the underlying DataFrame.

For the second example, we will use the map. Since we downloaded the KDD cup data, we know that it is a comma-separated value file, and so, one of the very easy things for us to do is to split each line by two commas, as follows:

```
split_file = raw_data.map(lambda line: line.split(","))
```

Let's analyze what is happening. We call the map function on raw_data. We feed it an anonymous lambda function called line, where we are splitting the line function by using ,. The result is a split file. Now, here the power of Spark really comes into play. Recall that, in the contains_normal. filter, when we called a function that forced Spark to calculate count, it took us a few minutes to come up with the correct results. If we perform the map function, it is going to have the same effect, because there are going to be millions of lines of data that we need to map through. And so, one of the ways to quickly preview whether our mapping function runs correctly is if we can materialize a few lines instead of the whole file.

To do this, we can use the take function that we have used before, as demonstrated in the following screenshot:

```
>>> split_file.take(5)
[['0', 'tcp', 'http', 'SF', '215', '45076', '0', '0', '0', '0', '0', '1', '0', '0', '0', '0', '0', '0', '0', '0
', '0', '0', '1', '1', '0.00', '0.00', '0.00', '0.00', '1.00', '0.00', '0.00', '0', '0', '0.00', '0.00', '0.00
, '0.00', '0.00', '0.00', '0.00', '0.00', 'normal.'], ['0', 'tcp', 'http', 'SF', '162', '4528', '0', '0', '0',
'0', '0', '1', '0', '0', '0', '0', '0', '0', '0', '0', '2', '2', '0.00', '0.00', '0.00', '0.00', '1.0
0', '0.00', '0.00', '1', '1', '1.00', '0.00', '1.00', '0.00', '0.00', '0.00', '0.00', '0.00', 'normal.'], ['0',
'tcp', 'http', 'SF', '236', '1228', '0', '0', '0', '0', '0', '1', '0', '0', '0', '0', '0', '0', '0', '0', '0',
'0', '1', '1', '0.00', '0.00', '0.00', '0.00', '1.00', '0.00', '0.00', '2', '2', '1.00', '0.00', '0.50', '0.00
', '0.00', '0.00', '0.00', '0.00', 'normal.'], ['0', 'tcp', 'http', 'SF', '233', '2032', '0', '0', '0', '0', '0
', '1', '0', '0', '0', '0', '0', '0', '0', '0', '2', '2', '0.00', '0.00', '0.00', '0.00', '1.00', '0.
00', '0.00', '3', '3', '1.00', '0.00', '0.33', '0.00', '0.00', '0.00', '0.00', '0.00', 'normal.'], ['0', 'tcp',
'http', 'SF', '239', '486', '0', '0', '0', '0', '0', '1', '0', '0', '0', '0', '0', '0', '0', '0', '0', '3
', '3', '0.00', '0.00', '0.00', '0.00', '1.00', '0.00', '0.00', '4', '4', '1.00', '0.00', '0.25', '0.00', '0.00
', '0.00', '0.00', '0.00', 'normal.']]
>>>
```

This might take a few seconds because we are only taking five lines, which is our splits and is actually quite manageable. If we look at this sample output, we can understand that our map function has been created successfully. The last thing we can do is to call collect() on raw data as follows:

```
raw_data.collect()
```

This is designed to move all of the raw data from Spark's RDD data structure into the memory.

Summary

In this chapter, we learned how to load data on Spark RDDs and also covered parallelization with Spark RDDs. We had a brief overview of the UCI machine learning repository before loading the data. We had an overview of the basic RDD operations, and also checked the functions from the official documentation.

In the next chapter, we will cover big data cleaning and data wrangling.

3
Big Data Cleaning and Wrangling with Spark Notebooks

In this chapter, we will learn about big data cleaning and wrangling with Spark Notebooks. We will also look at how using Spark on a Notebook application allows us to use RDDs effectively. We will use Spark Notebooks for quick iteration of ideas and carry out sampling/filtering RDDs to pick out relevant data points. We will also learn how to split datasets and create new combinations with set operations.

In this chapter, we will discuss the following topics:

- Using Spark Notebooks for quick iteration of ideas
- Sampling/filtering RDDs to pick out relevant data points
- Splitting datasets and creating some new combinations

Using Spark Notebooks for quick iteration of ideas

In this section, we will answer the following questions:

- What are Spark Notebooks?
- How do you start Spark Notebooks?
- How do you use Spark Notebooks?

Let's start with setting up a Jupyter Notebook-like environment for Spark. Spark Notebook is just an interactive and reactive data science environment that uses Scala and Spark.

If we view the GitHub page (https://github.com/spark-notebook/spark-notebook), we can see that what the Notebooks do is actually very straightforward, as shown in the following screenshot:

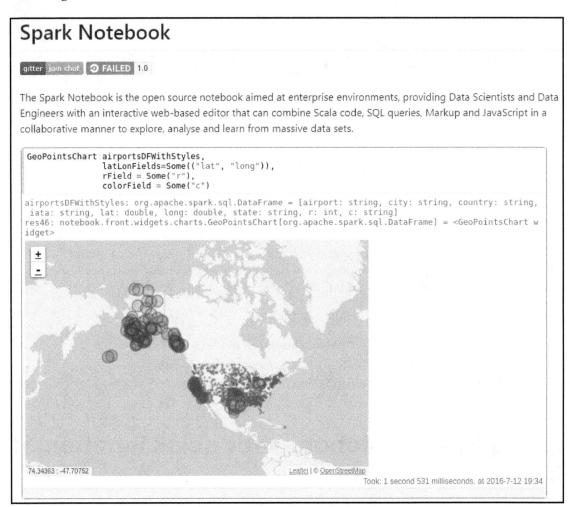

If we look at a Spark Notebook, we can see that they look very much like what Python developers use, which is Jupyter Notebooks. You have a text box allowing you to enter some code, and then you execute the code below the text box, which is similar to a Notebook format. This allows us to perform a reproducible analysis with Apache Spark and the big data ecosystem.

So, we can use Spark Notebooks as it is, and all we need to do is go to the Spark Notebook website and click on **Quick Start** to get the Notebook started, as shown in the following screenshot:

ℭ Reactive

All components in the Spark Notebook are dynamic and reactive.

The Spark Notebook comes with dynamic charts and most (if not all) components can be listened for and can react to events. This is very helpful in many cases, for example:

- data entering the system live at runtime
- visually plots of events
- multiple interconnected visual components Dynamic and reactive components mean that you don't have write the html, js, server code just for basic use cases.

Quick Start

Go to Quick Start for our 5-minutes guide to get up and running with the Spark Notebook.

C'mon on to Gitter to discuss things, to get some help, or to start contributing!

Learn more

We need to make sure that we are running Java 7. We can see that the setup steps are also mentioned in the documentation, as shown in the following screenshot:

Documentation

Quick Start Guide

Start using the Spark Notebook in less than 5 minutes? Take these steps:

Requirements:

- Make sure you are running at least Java 7

Steps

- Go to spark-notebook.io
  - Choose your release, spark version and additional packages according to your specific needs
    - Read more on: Using Releases
  - If trying Spark for the first time, pick the latest release
- Download one of the packaged builds (TGZ or ZIP)
- Extract the file somewhere convenient
- Open a terminal/command window
- Change to the root directory of the expanded distribution
- Execute the command `bin/spark-notebook` (*NIX) or `bin\spark-notebook` (Windows)
- Open your browser to localhost:9001

The main website for Spark Notebook is `spark-notebook.io`, where we can see many options. A few of them have been shown in the following screenshot:

tgz		deb		zip	
Notebook 0.8.3		**Notebook 0.7.0-pre2**		**Notebook 0.8.3**	
Scala 2.11	Scala 2.10	Scala 2.11	Scala 2.10	Scala 2.11	Scala 2.10
Spark 2.2.2 and Hadoop	Spark 2.2.2 and Hadoop	Spark 1.6.3 and Hadoop	Spark 1.6.0 and Hadoop	Spark 2.2.2 and Hadoop	Spark 2.2.2 and Hadoop
○ 2.7.2 parquet	○ 2.7.2 parquet	○ 2.7.2	○ 2.6.0 hive parquet	○ 2.6.0 hive parquet ○ 2.7.2 hive parquet ○ 2.7.2 parquet ○ 2.7.3 hive parquet	○ 1.0.3 parquet ○ 2.7.2 parquet

We can download the TAR file and unzip it. You can use Spark Notebook, but we will be using Jupyter Notebook in this book. So, going back to the Jupyter environment, we can look at the PySpark-accompanying code files. In `Chapter 3` Notebook we have included a convenient way for us to set up the environment variables to get PySpark working with Jupyter, as shown in the following screenshot:

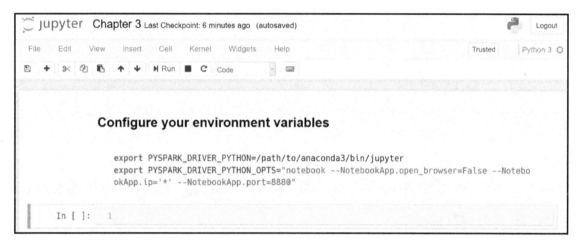

First, we need to create two new **environment variables** in our environments. If you are using Linux, you can use Bash RC. If you are using Windows, all you need to do is to change and edit your system **environment variables**. There are multiple tutorials online to help you do this. What we want to do here is to edit or include the `PYSPARK_DRIVER_PYTHON` variable and point it to your Jupyter Notebook installation. If you are on Anaconda, you probably would be pointed to the Anaconda Jupyter Bash file. Since we are on WinPython, I have pointed it to my WinPython Jupyter Notebook Bash file. The second **environment variable** we want to export is simply `PYSPARK_DRIVER_PYTHON_OPTS`.

One of the suggestions is that we include the Notebook folder and the Notebook app in the options, ask it not to open in the browser, and tell it what port to bind to. In practice, if you are on Windows and WinPython environments then you don't really need this line here, and you can simply skip it. After this has been done, simply restart your PySpark from a command line. What will happen is that, instead of having the console that we have seen before, it directly launches into a Jupyter Notebook instance, and, furthermore, we can use Spark and SparkContext variables as in Jupyter Notebook. So, let's test it out as follows:

```
sc
```

We instantly get access to our `SparkContext` that tells us that Spark is version `2.3.3`, our `Master` is at `local`, and the `AppName` is the Python SparkShell (`PySparkShell`), as shown in the following code snippet:

```
SparkContext
Spark UI
Version
 v2.3.3
Master
 local[*]
AppName
 PySparkShell
```

So, now we know how we create a Notebook-like environment in Jupyter. In the next section, we will look at sampling and filtering RDDs to pick out relevant data points.

Sampling/filtering RDDs to pick out relevant data points

In this section, we will look at sampling and filtering RDDs to pick up relevant data points. This is a very powerful concept that allows us to circumvent the limitations of big data and perform our calculations on a particular sample.

Let's now check how sampling not only speeds up our calculations, but also gives us a good approximation of the statistic that we are trying to calculate. To do this, we first import the `time` library as follows:

```
from time import time
```

The next thing we want to do is look at lines or data points in the KDD database that contains the word `normal`:

```
raw_data = sc.textFile("./kdd.data.gz")
```

We need to create a sample of `raw_data`. We will store the sample into the `sample,` variable, and we're sampling from `raw_data` without replacement. We're sampling 10% of the data, and we're providing `42` as our random seed:

```
sampled = raw_data.sample(False, 0.1, 42)
```

The next thing to do is to chain some `map` and `filter` functions, as we do normally if we are dealing with unsampled datasets:

```
contains_normal_sample = sampled.map(lambda x: x.split(",")).filter(lambda
x: "normal" in x)
```

Next, we need to time how long it would take for us to count the number of rows in the sample:

```
t0 = time()
num_sampled = contains_normal_sample.count()
duration = time() - t0
```

We issue the count statement here. As you know from the previous section, this is going to trigger all the calculations in PySpark as defined in `contains_normal_sample`, and we're recording the time before the sample count happens. We are also recording the time after the sample count happens, so we can see how long it takes when we're looking at a sample. Once this is done, let's take a look at how long the `duration` was in the following code snippet:

```
duration
```

The output will be as follows:

```
23.724565505981445
```

It took us 23 seconds to run this operation over 10% of the data. Now, let's look at what happens if we run the same transform over all of the data:

```
contains_normal = raw_data.map(lambda x: x.split(",")).filter(lambda x:
"normal" in x)
t0 = time()
num_sampled = contains_normal.count()
duration = time() - t0
```

Let's take a look at the `duration` again:

```
duration
```

This will provide the following output:

```
36.51565098762512
```

There is a small difference, as we are comparing 36.5 seconds to 23.7 seconds. However, this difference becomes much larger as your dataset becomes much more varied, and the amount of data you're dealing with becomes much more complex. The great thing about this is that, if you are usually doing big data, verifying whether your answers make sense with a small sample of the data can help you catch bugs much earlier on.

The last thing to look at is how we can use `takeSample`. All we need to do is use the following code:

```
data_in_memory = raw_data.takeSample(False, 10, 42)
```

As we've learned earlier, when we present the new functions we call `takeSample`, and it will give us 10 items with a random seed of 42, which we will now put into memory. Now that this data is in memory, we can call the same `map` and `filter` functions using native Python methods as follows:

```
contains_normal_py = [line.split(",") for line in data_in_memory if
"normal" in line]
len(contains_normal_py)
```

The output will be as follows:

```
1
```

We have now finished calculating our `contains_normal` function by bringing `data_in_memory`. This is a great illustration of the power of PySpark.

We originally took a sample of 10,000 data points, and it crashed the machine. So here, we will take these ten data points to see if it contains the word `normal`.

We can see that the calculation is completed in the previous code block, and it took longer and used more memory than if we were doing it in PySpark. And that's why we use Spark, because Spark allows us to parallelize any big datasets and operate it on it using a parallel fashion, which means that we can do more with less memory and with less time. In the next section, we're going to talk about splitting datasets and creating new combinations with set operations.

Splitting datasets and creating some new combinations

In this section, we are going to look at splitting datasets and creating new combinations with set operations. We're going to learn subtracts, and Cartesian ones in particular.

Let's go back to `Chapter 3` of the Jupyter Notebook that we've been looking at lines in the datasets that contain the word `normal`. Let's try to get all the lines that don't contain the word `normal`. One way is to use the `filter` function to look at lines that don't have `normal` in it. But, we can use something different in PySpark: a function called `subtract` to take the entire dataset and subtract the data that contains the word `normal`. Let's have a look at the following snippet:

```
normal_sample = sampled.filter(lambda line: "normal." in line)
```

We can then obtain interactions or data points that don't contain the word `normal` by subtracting the `normal` ones from the entire sample as follows:

```
non_normal_sample = sampled.subtract(normal_sample)
```

We take the `normal` sample and we subtract it from the entire sample, which is 10% of the entire dataset. Let's issue some counts as follows:

```
sampled.count()
```

This will give us the following output:

```
490705
```

As you can see, 10% of the dataset gives us `490705` data points, and within it, we have a number of data points containing the word `normal`. To find out its count, write the following code:

```
normal_sample.count()
```

This will give us the following output:

```
97404
```

So, here we have `97404` data points. If we count the on normal samples because we're simply subtracting one sample from another, the count should be roughly just below 400,000 data points, because we have 490,000 data points minus 97,000 data points, which should result in something like 390,000. Let's see what happens using the following code snippet:

```
non_normal_sample.count()
```

This will give us the following output:

```
393301
```

As expected, it returned a value of 393301, which validates our assumption that subtracting the data points containing normal gives us all the non-normal data points.

Let's now discuss the other function, called cartesian. This allows us to give all the combinations between the distinct values of two different features. Let's see how this works in the following code snippet:

```
feature_1 = sampled.map(lambda line: line.split(",")).map(lambda features:
features[1]).distinct()
```

Here, we're splitting the line function by using , . So, we will split the values that are comma-separated—for all the features that we come up with after splitting, we take the first feature, and we find all the distinct values of that column. We can repeat this for the second feature as follows:

```
feature_2 = sampled.map(lambda line: line.split(",")).map(lambda features:
features[2]).distinct()
```

And so, we now have two features. We can look at the actual items in feature_1 andfeature_2 as follows, by issuing the collect() call that we saw earlier:

```
f1 = feature_1.collect()
f2 = feature_2.collect()
```

Let's look at each one as follows:

```
f1
```

This will provide the following outcome:

```
['tcp', 'udp', 'icmp']
```

So, f1 has three values; let's check for f2 as follows:

```
f2
```

This will provide us with the following output:

```
In [29]:    1 f2
Out[29]: ['http',
          'finger',
          'auth',
          'domain_u',
          'smtp',
          'ftp',
          'telnet',
          'eco_i',
          'ntp_u',
          'ecr_i',
          'other',
          'private',
          'pop_3',
```

f2 has a lot more values, and we can use the cartesian function to collect all the combinations between f1 and f2 as follows:

```
len(feature_1.cartesian(feature_2).collect())
```

This will give us the following output:

```
198
```

This is how we use the cartesian function to find the Cartesian product between two features. In this chapter, we looked at Spark Notebooks; sampling, filtering, and splitting datasets; and creating new combinations with set operations.

Summary

In this chapter, we looked at Spark Notebooks for quick iterations. We then used sampling or filtering to pick out relevant data points. We also learned how to split datasets and create new combinations with set operations.

In the next chapter, we will cover aggregating and summarizing data into useful reports.

4
Aggregating and Summarizing Data into Useful Reports

In this chapter, we will learn how to aggregate and summarize data into useful reports. We will learn how to calculate averages with `map` and `reduce` functions, perform faster average computation, and use pivot tables with key-value pair data points.

In this chapter, we will cover the following topics:

- Calculating averages with `map` and `reduce`
- Faster average computations with aggregate
- Pivot tabling with key-value paired data points

Calculating averages with map and reduce

We will be answering the following three main questions in this section:

- How do we calculate averages?
- What is a map?
- What is reduce?

You can check the documentation at `https://spark.apache.org/docs/latest/api/python/pyspark.html?highlight=map#pyspark.RDD.map`.

The `map` function takes two arguments, one of which is optional. The first argument to `map` is `f`, which is a function that gets applied to the RDD throughout by the `map` function. The second argument, or parameter, is the `preservesPartitioning` parameter, which is `False` by default.

If we look at the documentation, it says that map simply returns a new RDD by applying a function to each element of this RDD, and obviously, this function refers to f that we feed into the map function itself. There's a very simple example in the documentation, where it says if we parallelize an rdd method that contains a list of three characters, b, a, and c, and we map a function that creates a tuple of each element, then we'll create a list of three-tuples, where the original character is placed in the first elements of the tuple, and the 1 integer is placed in the second as follows:

```
rdd =  sc.paralleize(["b", "a", "c"])
sorted(rdd.map(lambda x: (x, 1)).collect())
```

This will give us the following output:

```
[('a', 1), ('b', 1), ('c', 1)]
```

The reduce function takes only one argument, which is f. f is a function to reduce a list into one number. From a technical point of view, the specified commutative and associative binary operator reduces the elements of this RDD.

Let's take an example using the KDD data we have been using. We launch our Jupyter Notebook instance that links to a Spark instance, as we have done previously. We then create a raw_data variable by loading a kddcup.data.gz text file from the local disk as follows:

```
raw_data = sc.textFile("./kddcup.data.gz")
```

The next thing to do is to split this file into csv, and then we will filter for rows where feature 41 includes the word normal:

```
csv = raw_data.map(lambda x: x.split(","))
normal_data = csv.filter(lambda x: x[41]=="normal.")
```

Then we use the map function to convert this data into an integer, and then, finally, we can use the reduce function to compute the total_duration, and then we can print the total_duration as follows:

```
duration = normal_data.map(lambda x: int(x[0]))
total_duration = duration.reduce(lambda x, y: x+y)
total_duration
```

We will then get the following output:

```
211895753
```

The next thing to do is to divide `total_duration` by the counts of the data as follows:

```
total_duration/(normal_data.count())
```

This will give us the following output:

```
217.82472416710442
```

And after a little computation, we would have created two counts using `map` and `reduce`. We have just learned how we can calculate averages with PySpark, and what the `map` and `reduce` functions are in PySpark.

Faster average computations with aggregate

In the previous section, we saw how we can use `map` and `reduce` to calculate averages. Let's now look at faster average computations with the `aggregate` function. You can refer to the documentation mentioned in the previous section.

The `aggregate` is a function that takes three arguments, none of which are optional.

The first one is the `zeroValue` argument, where we put in the base case of the aggregated results.

The second argument is the sequential operator (`seqOp`), which allows you to stack and aggregate values on top of `zeroValue`. You can start with `zeroValue`, and the `seqOp` function that you feed into `aggregate` takes values from your RDD, and stacks or aggregates it on top of `zeroValue`.

The last argument is `combOp`, which stands for combination operation, where we simply take the `zeroValue` argument that is now aggregated through the `seqOp` argument, and combine it into one value so that we can use this to conclude the aggregation.

So, here we are aggregating the elements of each partition and then the results for all the partitions using a combined function and a neutral zero value. Here, we have two things to note:

1. The `op` function is allowed to modify `t1`, but it should not modify `t2`
2. The first function `seqOp` can return a different result type `U`

In this case, we all need one operation for merging a `T` into `U`, and one operation for merging the two Us.

Let's go to our Jupyter Notebook to check how this is done. `aggregate` allows us to calculate both the total duration and the count at the same time. We call the `duration_count` function. We then take `normal_data` and we aggregate it. Remember that there are three arguments to aggregate. The first one is the initial value; that is, the zero value, `(0, 0)`. The second one is a sequential operation, as follows:

```
duration_count = duration.aggregate(
    (0,0),
    (lambda db, new_value: (db[0] + new_value, db[1] + 1))
)
```

We need to specify a `lambda` function with two arguments. The first argument is the current accumulator, or the aggregator, or what can also be called a database (`db`). Then, we have the second argument in our `lambda` function as `new_value`, or the current value we're processing in the RDD. We simply want to do the right thing to the database, so to say, where we know that our database looks like a tuple with the sum of duration on the first element and the count on the second element. Here, we know that our database looks like a tuple, where the sum of duration is the first element, and the count is the second element. Whenever we look at a new value, we need to add the new value to the current running total and add 1 to the current running counts.

The running total is the first element, `db[0]`. And we then simply need to add 1 to the second element `db[1]`, which is the count. That's the sequential operation.

Every time we get a `new_value`, as shown in the previous code block, we simply add it to the running total. And, because we've added `new_value` to the running total, we need to increment the counts by 1. Secondly, we need to put in the combinator operation. Now, we simply need to combine the respective elements of two separate databases, `db1` and `db2`, as follows:

```
duration_count = duration.aggregate(
    (0,0),
    (lambda db, new_value: (db[0] + new_value, db[1] + 1)),
    (lambda db1, db2: (db1[0] + db2[0], db1[1] + db2[1]))
)
```

Since the duration counts is a tuple that collects our total duration on the first element, and counts how many durations we looked at in the second element, computing the average is very simple. We need to divide the first element by the second element as follows:

```
duration_count[0]/duration_count[1]
```

This will give us the following output:

```
217.82472416710442
```

You can see that it returns the same results as we saw in the previous section, which is great. In the next section, we are going to look at pivot tabling with key-value paired data points.

Pivot tabling with key-value paired data points

Pivot tables are very simple and easy to use. What we are going to do is use big datasets, such as the KDD cup dataset, and group certain values by certain keys.

For example, we have a dataset of people and their favorite fruits. We want to know how many people have apple as their favorite fruit, so we will group the number of people, which is the value, against a key, which is the fruit. This is the simple concept of a pivot table.

We can use the map function to move the KDD datasets into a key-value pair paradigm. We map feature 41 of the dataset using a lambda function in the kv key value, and we append the value as follows:

```
kv = csv.map(lambda x: (x[41], x))
kv.take(1)
```

We use feature 41 as the key, and the value is the data point, which is x. We can use the take function to take one of these transformed rows to see how it looks.

Let's now try something similar to the previous example. To figure out the total duration against each type of value that is present in feature 41, we can use the map function again and simply take the 41 feature as our key. We can take the float of the first number in the data point as our value. We will use the reduceByKey function to reduce each duration by its key.

So, instead of just reducing all of the data points regardless of which key they belong to, reduceByKey reduces duration numbers depending on which key it is associated with. You can view the documentation at https://spark.apache.org/docs/latest/api/python/pyspark.html?highlight=map#pyspark.RDD.reduceByKey. reduceByKey merges the values for each key using an associative and commutative reduce function. It performs local merging on each mapper before sending the results to the reducer, which is similar to a combiner in MapReduce.

The `reduceByKey` function simply takes one argument. We will be using the `lambda` function. We take two different durations and add them together, and PySpark is smart enough to apply this reduction function depending on a key, as follows:

```
kv_duration = csv.map(lambda x: (x[41], float(x[0]))).reduceByKey(lambda x,
y: x+y)
kv_duration.collect()
```

The resulting output is shown in the following screenshot:

```
[('normal.', 211895753.0),
 ('buffer_overflow.', 2751.0)
 ('loadmodule.', 326.0),
 ('perl.', 124.0),
 ('neptune.', 2.0),
 ('smurf.', 0.0),
 ('guess_passwd.', 144.0),
 ('pod.', 0.0),
 ('teardrop.', 0.0),
 ('portsweep.', 24257982.0),
 ('ipsweep.', 13049.0),
 ('land.', 0.0),
 ('ftp_write.', 259.0),
 ('back.', 284.0),
 ('imap.', 72.0),
 ('satan.', 500.0),
 ('phf.', 18.0),
 ('nmap.', 0.0),
 ('multihop.', 1288.0),
 ('warezmaster.', 301.0),
 ('warezclient.', 627563.0),
 ('spy.', 636.0),
 ('rootkit.', 1008.0)]
```

If we collect the key-value duration data, we can see that the duration is collected by the value that appears in feature 41. If we are using pivot tables in Excel, there is a convenience function that is the `countByKey` function, which does the exact same thing, demonstrated as follows:

```
kv.countByKey()
```

This will give us the following output:

```
defaultdict(int,
            {'back.': 2203,
             'buffer_overflow.': 30,
             'ftp_write.': 8,
             'guess_passwd.': 53,
             'imap.': 12,
             'ipsweep.': 12481,
             'land.': 21,
             'loadmodule.': 9,
             'multihop.': 7,
             'neptune.': 1072017,
             'nmap.': 2316,
             'normal.': 972781,
             'perl.': 3,
             'phf.': 4,
             'pod.': 264,
             'portsweep.': 10413,
             'rootkit.': 10,
             'satan.': 15892,
```

You can see that calling the `kv.countByKey()` function is the same as calling the `reduceByKey` function, preceded by a mapping from the key to the duration.

Summary

In this chapter, we have learned how to calculate averages with `map` and `reduce`. We also learned faster average computations with `aggregate`. Finally, we learned that pivot tables allow us to aggregate data based on different values of features, and that, with pivot tables in PySpark, we can leverage handy functions, such as `reducedByKey` or `countByKey`.

In the next chapter, we will learn about MLlib, which involves machine learning, which is a very hot topic.

Powerful Exploratory Data Analysis with MLlib

5

In this chapter, we will explore Spark's capability to perform regression tasks with models such as linear regression and **support-vector machines** (**SVMs**). We will learn how to compute summary statistics with MLlib, and discover correlations in datasets using Pearson and Spearman correlations. We will also test our hypothesis on large datasets.

We will cover the following topics:

- Computing summary statistics with MLlib
- Using the Pearson and Spearman methods to discover correlations
- Testing our hypotheses on large datasets

Computing summary statistics with MLlib

In this section, we will be answering the following questions:

- What are summary statistics?
- How do we use MLlib to create summary statistics?

MLlib is the machine learning library that comes with Spark. There has been a recent new development that allows us to use Spark's data-processing capabilities to pipe into machine learning capabilities native to Spark. This means that we can use Spark not only to ingest, collect, and transform data, but we can also analyze and use it to build machine learning models on the PySpark platform, which allows us to have a more seamless deployable solution.

Summary statistics are a very simple concept. We are familiar with average, or standard deviation, or the variance of a particular variable. These are summary statistics of a dataset. The reason why it's called a summary statistic is that it gives you a summary of something via a certain statistic. For example, when we talk about the average of a dataset, we're summarizing one characteristic of that dataset, and that characteristic is the average.

Let's check how to compute summary statistics in Spark. The key factor here is the colStats function. The colStats function computes the column-wise summary statistics for an rdd input. The colStats function accepts one parameter, that is rdd, and it allows us to compute different summary statistics using Spark.

Let's look at the code in the Jupyter Notebook (available at https://github.com/ PacktPublishing/Hands-On-Big-Data-Analytics-with-PySpark/tree/master/Chapter05) for this chapter in Chapter5.ipynb. We will first collect the data from the kddcup.data.gz text file and pipe this into the raw_data variable as follows:

```
raw_data = sc.textFile("./kddcup.data.gz")
```

The kddcup.data file is a **comma-separated value (CSV)** file. We have to split this data by the , character and put it in the csv variable as follows:

```
csv = raw_data.map(lambda x: x.split(","))
```

Let's take the first feature x[0] of the data file; this feature represents the duration, that is, aspects of the data. We will transform it into an integer here, and also wrap it in a list as follows:

```
duration = csv.map(lambda x: [int(x[0])])
```

This helps us do summary statistics over multiple variables, and not just one of them. To activate the colStats function, we need to import the Statistics package, as shown in the following snippet:

```
from pyspark.mllib.stat import Statistics
```

This Statistics package is a sub package of pyspark.mllib.stat. Now, we need to call the colStats function in the Statistics package and feed it some data. Here, we are talking about the duration data from the dataset and we're feeding the summary statistics into the summary variable:

```
summary = Statistics.colStats(duration)
```

To access different summary statistics, such as the mean, standard deviation, and so on, we can call the functions of the `summary` objects, and access different summary statistics. For example, we can access the `mean`, and since we have only one feature in our `duration` dataset, we can index it by the `00` index, and we'll get the mean of the dataset as follows:

```
summary.mean()[0]
```

This will give us the following output:

```
47.97930249928637
```

Similarly, if we import the `sqrt` function from the Python standard library, we can create the standard deviation of the durations seen in the datasets, as demonstrated in the following code snippet:

```
from math import sqrt
sqrt(summary.variance()[0])
```

This will give us the following output:

```
707.746472305374
```

If we don't index the summary statistics with `[0]`, we can see that `summary.max()` and `summary.min()` gives us back an array, of which the first element is the summary statistic that we desire, as shown in the following code snippet:

```
summary.max()
array([58329.]) #output
summary.min()
array([0.])   #output
```

Using Pearson and Spearman correlations to discover correlations

In this section, we will look at two different ways of computing correlations in your datasets, and these two methods are called Pearson and Spearman correlations.

The Pearson correlation

The Pearson correlation coefficient shows us how two different variables vary at the same time, and then adjusts it for how much they vary. This is probably one of the most popular ways to compute a correlation if you have a dataset.

The Spearman correlation

Spearman's rank correlation is not the default correlation calculation that is built into PySpark, but it is very useful. The Spearman correlation coefficient is the Pearson correlation coefficient between the ranked variables. Using different ways of looking at correlation gives us more dimensions of understanding on how correlation works. Let's look at how we calculate this in PySpark.

Computing Pearson and Spearman correlations

To understand this, let's assume that we are taking the first three numeric variables from our dataset. For this, we want to access the `csv` variable that we defined previously, where we simply split `raw_data` using a comma (,). We will consider only the first three columns that are numeric. We will not take anything that contains words; we're only interested in features that are purely based on numbers. In our case, in `kddcup.data`, the first feature is indexed at 0; feature 5 and feature 6 are indexed at 4 and 5, respectively which are the numeric variables that we have. We use a `lambda` function to take all three of these into a list and put it into the `metrics` variable:

```
metrics = csv.map(lambda x: [x[0], x[4], x[5]])
Statistics.corr(metrics, method="spearman")
```

This will give us the following output:

```
array([[1.         ,  0.01419628,  0.29918926],
       [0.01419628,  1.         , -0.16793059],
       [0.29918926, -0.16793059,  1.         ]])
```

In the *Computing summary statistics with MLlib* section, we simply took the first feature into a list and created a list with a length of one. Here, we're taking three quantities of three variables into the same list. Now, each list has a length of three.

To compute the correlations, we call the `corr` method on the `metrics` variable and specify the `method` as `"spearman"`. PySpark would give us a very simple matrix telling us the correlation between the variables. In our example, the third variable in our `metrics` variable is more correlated than the second variable.

If we run `corr` on `metrics` again, but specify that the method is `pearson`, then it gives us Pearson correlations. So, let's examine why we need to be qualified as the data scientist or machine learning researcher to call these two simple functions and simply change the value of the second parameter. A lot of machine learning and data science revolves around our understanding of statistics, understanding how data behaves, an understanding of how machine learning models are grounded, and what gives them their predictive power.

So, as a machine learning practitioner or a data scientist, we simply use PySpark as a big calculator. When we use a calculator, we never complain that the calculator is simple to use—in fact, it helps us to complete the goal in a more straightforward way. It is the same case with PySpark; once we move from the data engineering side to the MLlib side, we will notice that the code gets incrementally easier. It tries to hide the complexity of the mathematics underneath it, but we need to understand the difference between different correlations, and we also need to know how and when to use them.

Testing our hypotheses on large datasets

In this section, we will look at hypothesis testing, and also learn how to test the hypotheses using PySpark. Let's look at one particular type of hypothesis testing that is implemented in PySpark. This form of hypothesis testing is called Pearson's chi-square test. Chi-square tests how likely it is that the differences in the two datasets are there by chance.

For example, if we had a retail store without any footfall, and suddenly you get footfall, how likely is it that this is random, or is there even any statistically significant difference in the level of visitors that we are getting now in comparison to before? The reason why this is called the chi-square test is that the test itself references the chi-square distributions. You can refer to online documentation to understand more about chi-square distributions.

There are three variations within Pearson's chi-square test. We will check whether the observed datasets are distributed differently than in a theoretical dataset.

Let's see how we can implement this. Let's start by importing the `Vectors` package from `pyspark.mllib.linalg`. Using this vector, we're going to create a dense vector of the visitor frequencies by day in our store.

Let's imagine that the frequencies go from 0.13 an hour to 0.61, 0.8, and 0.5, finally ending on Friday at 0.3. So, we are putting these visitor frequencies into the `visitors_freq` variable. Since we're using PySpark, it is very simple for us to run a chi-square test from the `Statistics` package, which we have already imported as follows:

```
from pyspark.mllib.linalg import Vectors
visitors_freq = Vectors.dense(0.13, 0.61, 0.8, 0.5, 0.3)
print(Statistics.chiSqTest(visitors_freq))
```

By running the chi-square test, the `visitors_freq` variable gives us a bunch of useful information, as demonstrated in the following screenshot:

```
Chi squared test summary:
method: pearson
degrees of freedom = 4
statistic = 0.5852136752136753
pValue = 0.9646925263439344
No presumption against null hypothesis: observed follows the same distribution as expected..
```

The preceding output shows the chi-square test summary. We've used the `pearson` method, where there are 4 degrees of freedom in our Pearson chi-square test, and the statistics are 0.585, which means that the `pValue` is 0.964. This results in no presumption against the null hypothesis. In this way, the observed data follows the same distribution as expected, which means our visitors are not actually different. This gives us a good understanding of hypothesis testing.

Summary

In this chapter, we learned summary statistics and computing the summary statistics with MLlib. We also learned about Pearson and Spearman correlations, and how we can discover these correlations in our datasets using PySpark. Finally, we learned one particular way of performing hypothesis testing, which is called the Pearson chi-square test. We then used PySpark's hypothesis-testing functions to test our hypotheses on large datasets.

In the next chapter, we're going to look at putting the structure on our big data with Spark SQL.

6
Putting Structure on Your Big Data with SparkSQL

In this chapter, we'll learn how to manipulate DataFrames with Spark SQL schemas, and use the Spark DSL to build queries for structured data operations. By now we have already learned to get big data into the Spark Environment using RDDs and carried out multiple operations on that big data. Let us now look that how to manipulate our DataFrames and build queries for structured data operations.

In particular, we will cover the following topics:

- Manipulating DataFrames with Spark SQL schemas
- Using Spark DSL to build queries

Manipulating DataFrames with Spark SQL schemas

In this section, we will learn more about DataFrames and learn how to use Spark SQL.

The Spark SQL interface is very simple. For this reason, taking away labels means that we are in unsupervised learning territory. Also, Spark has great support for clustering and dimensionality reduction algorithms. We can tackle learning problems effectively by using Spark SQL to give big data a structure.

Let's take a look at the code that we will be using in our Jupyter Notebook. To maintain consistency, we will be using the same KDD cup data:

1. We will first type `textFile` into a `raw_data` variable as follows:

   ```
   raw_data = sc.textFile("./kddcup.data.gz")
   ```

2. What's new here is that we are importing two new packages from `pyspark.sql`:
   - Row
   - SQLContext

3. The following code shows us how to import these packages:

   ```
   from pyspark.sql import Row, SQLContext
   sql_context = SQLContext(sc)
   csv = raw_data.map(lambda l: l.split(","))
   ```

   Using `SQLContext`, we create a new `sql_context` variable that holds the object of the `SQLContext` variable created by PySpark. As we're using `SparkContext` to start this `SQLContext` variable, we need to pipe in `sc` as the first parameter of the `SQLContext` creator. After this, we need to take our `raw_data` variable and map it with the `l.split` lambda function to create an object that holds our **comma-separated values** (**CSV**).

4. We'll leverage our new important `Row` objects to create a new object that has defined labels. This is to label our datasets by what feature we are looking at, as follows:

   ```
   rows = csv.map(lambda p: Row(duration=int(p[0]), protocol=p[1],
   service=p[2]))
   ```

In the preceding code, we've taken our comma-separated values (csv), and we've created a Row object that takes the first feature, called duration; the second feature, called protocol; and the third feature, called service. This directly corresponds to our labels in the actual datasets.

5. Now, we can create a new DataFrame by calling the createDataFrame function in our sql_context variable. To create this DataFrame, we need to feed in our row data objects, and the resulting object would be a DataFrame in df. After this, we need to register a temporary table. Here, we are just calling it rdd. By doing this, we can now use ordinary SQL syntax to query the content in this temporary table that is constructed by our rows:

```
df = sql_context.createDataFrame(rows)
df.registerTempTable("rdd")
```

6. In our example, we need to select the duration from rdd, which is a temporary table. The protocol we have selected here is equal to 'tcp', and the duration, which is our first feature in a row, is larger than 2000, as demonstrated in the following code snippet:

```
sql_context.sql("""SELECT duration FROM rdd WHERE protocol = 'tcp'
AND duration > 2000""")
```

7. Now, when we call the show function, it gives us every single data point that matches these criteria:

```
sql_context.sql("""SELECT duration FROM rdd WHERE protocol = 'tcp'
AND duration > 2000""").show()
```

8. We will then get the following output:

```
+--------+
|duration|
+--------+
|   12454|
|   10774|
|   13368|
|   10350|
|   10409|
|   14918|
|   10039|
|   15127|
|   25602|
|   13120|
|    2399|
|    6155|
```

```
|    11155|
|    12169|
|    15239|
|    10901|
|    15182|
|     9494|
|     7895|
|    11084|
+--------+
only showing top 20 rows
```

Using the preceding example, we can infer that we can use the `SQLContext` variable from the PySpark package to package our data in a SQL friendly format.

Therefore, not only does PySpark support using SQL syntax to query the data, but it can also use the Spark **domain-specific language** (**DSL**) to build queries for structured data operations.

Using Spark DSL to build queries

In this section, we will use Spark DSL to build queries for structured data operations:

1. In the following command, we have used the same query as used earlier; this time expressed in the Spark DSL to illustrate and compare how using the Spark DSL is different, but achieves the same goal as our SQL is shown in the previous section:

   ```
   df.select("duration").filter(df.duration>2000).filter(df.protocol==
   "tcp").show()
   ```

   In this command, we first take the `df` object that we created in the previous section. We then select the duration by calling the `select` function and feeding in the `duration` parameter.

2. Next, in the preceding code snippet, we call the `filter` function twice, first by using `df.duration`, and the second time by using `df.protocol`. In the first instance, we are trying to see whether the duration is larger than `2000`, and in the second instance, we are trying to see whether the protocol is equal to `"tcp"`. We also need to append the `show` function at the very end of the command to get the same results, as shown in the following code block:

```
+--------+
|duration|
+--------+
|   12454|
|   10774|
|   13368|
|   10350|
|   10409|
|   14918|
|   10039|
|   15127|
|   25602|
|   13120|
|    2399|
|    6155|
|   11155|
|   12169|
|   15239|
|   10901|
|   15182|
|    9494|
|    7895|
|   11084|
+--------+
only showing top 20 rows
```

Here, we have the top 20 rows of the data points again that fit the description of the code used to get this result.

Summary

In this chapter, we covered Spark DSL and learned how to build queries. We also learned how to manipulate DataFrames with Spark SQL schemas, and then we used Spark DSL to build queries for structured data operations. Now that we have a good knowledge of Spark, let's look at a few tips, tricks, and techniques in Apache Spark in the following chapters.

In the next chapter, we will look at transformations and actions in an Apache Spark program.

Transformations and Actions

7

Transformations and actions are the main building blocks of an Apache Spark program. In this chapter, we will look at Spark transformations to defer computations and then look at which transformations should be avoided. We will then use the `reduce` and `reduceByKey` methods to carry out calculations from a dataset. We will then perform actions that trigger actual computations on graphs. By the end of this chapter, we will also have learned how to reuse the same `rdd` for different actions.

In this chapter, we will cover the following topics:

- Using Spark transformations to defer computations to a later time
- Avoiding transformations
- Using the `reduce` and `reduceByKey` methods to calculate the result
- Performing actions that trigger actual computations of our **Directed Acyclic Graph (DAG)**
- Reusing the same `rdd` for different actions

Using Spark transformations to defer computations to a later time

Let's first understand Spark DAG creation. We will be executing DAG by issuing the action and also deferring the decision about starting the job until the last possible moment to check what this possibility gives us.

Let's have a look at the code we will be using in this section.

First, we need to initialize Spark. Every test we carry out will be the same. We need to initialize it before we start using it, as shown in the following example:

```
class DeferComputations extends FunSuite {
val spark: SparkContext =
SparkSession.builder().master("local[2]").getOrCreate().sparkContext
```

Then, we will have the actual test. Here, `test` is called `should defer computation`. It is simple but shows a very powerful abstraction of Spark. We start by creating an `rdd` of `InputRecord`, as shown in the following example:

```
test("should defer computations") {
  //given
    val input = spark.makeRDD(
        List(InputRecord(userId = "A"),
            InputRecord(userId = "B")))
```

`InputRecord` is a case class that has a unique identifier, which is an optional argument.

It can be a random `uuid` if we are not supplying it and the required argument, that is, `userId`. The `InputRecord` will be used throughout this book for testing purposes. We have created two records of the `InputRecord` that we will apply a transformation on, as shown in the following example:

```
//when apply transformation
val rdd = input
    .filter(_.userId.contains("A"))
    .keyBy(_.userId)
.map(_._2.userId.toLowerCase)
//.... built processing graph lazy
```

We will only filter records that have `A` in the `userId` field. We will then transform it to the `keyBy(_.userId)` and then extract `userId` from value and map it `toLowerCase`. This is our `rdd`. So, here, we have only created DAG, which we have not executed yet. Let's assume that we have a complex program and we are creating a lot of those acyclic graphs before the actual logic.

The pros of Spark are that this is not executed until action is issued, but we can have some conditional logic. For example, we can get a fast path execution. Let's assume that we have `shouldExecutePartOfCode()`, which can check a configuration switch, or go to the rest service to calculate if the `rdd` calculation is still relevant, as shown in the following example:

```
if (shouldExecutePartOfCode()) {
    //rdd.saveAsTextFile("") ||
    rdd.collect().toList
  } else {
    //condition changed - don't need to evaluate DAG
  }
}
```

We have used simple methods for testing purposes that we are just returning `true` for, but, in real life, this could be complex logic:

```
private def shouldExecutePartOfCode(): Boolean = {
    //domain logic that decide if we still need to calculate
    true
    }
}
```

After it returns `true`, we can decide if we want to execute the DAG or not. If we want to, we can call `rdd.collect().toList` or `saveAsTextFile` to execute the `rdd`. Otherwise, we can have a fast path and decide that we are no longer interested in the input `rdd`. By doing this, only the graph will be created.

When we start the test, it will take some time to complete and return the following output:

```
"C:\Program Files\Java\jdk-12\bin\java.exe" "-javaagent:C:\Program
Files\JetBrains\IntelliJ IDEA 2018.3.5\lib\idea_rt.jar=50627:C:\Program
Files\JetBrains\IntelliJ IDEA 2018.3.5\bin" -Dfile.encoding=UTF-8 -
classpath C:\Users\Sneha\IdeaProjects\Chapter07\out\production\Chapter07
com.company.Main

Process finished with exit code 0
```

We can see that our test passed and we can conclude that it worked as expected. Now, let's look at some transformations that should be avoided.

Avoiding transformations

In this section, we will look at the transformations that should be avoided. Here, we will focus on one particular transformation.

We will start by understanding the `groupBy` API. Then, we will investigate data partitioning when using `groupBy`, and then we will look at what a skew partition is and why should we avoid skew partitions.

Here, we are creating a list of transactions. `UserTransaction` is another model class that includes `userId` and `amount`. The following code block shows a typical transaction where we are creating a list of five transactions:

```
test("should trigger computations using actions") {
 //given
 val input = spark.makeRDD(
     List(
          UserTransaction(userId = "A", amount = 1001),
          UserTransaction(userId = "A", amount = 100),
          UserTransaction(userId = "A", amount = 102),
          UserTransaction(userId = "A", amount = 1),
          UserTransaction(userId = "B", amount = 13)))
```

We have created four transactions for `userId = "A"`, and one for `userId = "B"`.

Now, let's consider that we want to coalesce transactions for a specific `userId` to have the list of transactions. We have an `input` that we are grouping by `userId`, as shown in the following example:

```
//when apply transformation
val rdd = input
    .groupBy(_.userId)
    .map(x => (x._1,x._2.toList))
    .collect()
    .toList
```

For every x element, we will create a tuple. The first element of a tuple is an ID, while the second element is an iterator of every transaction for that specific ID. We will transform it into a list using `toList`. Then, we will collect everything and assign it to `toList` to have our result. Let's assert the result. `rdd` should contain the same element as B, that is, the key and one transaction, and A, which has four transactions, as shown in the following code:

```
//then
rdd should contain theSameElementsAs List(
    ("B", List(UserTransaction("B", 13))),
```

```
    ("A", List(
        UserTransaction("A", 1001),
        UserTransaction("A", 100),
        UserTransaction("A", 102),
        UserTransaction("A", 1))
    )
  )
 }
}
```

Let's start this test and check if this behaves as expected. We get the following output:

```
"C:\Program Files\Java\jdk-12\bin\java.exe" "-javaagent:C:\Program
Files\JetBrains\IntelliJ IDEA 2018.3.5\lib\idea_rt.jar=50822:C:\Program
Files\JetBrains\IntelliJ IDEA 2018.3.5\bin" -Dfile.encoding=UTF-8 -
classpath C:\Users\Sneha\IdeaProjects\Chapter07\out\production\Chapter07
com.company.Main

Process finished with exit code 0
```

At first glance, it has passed and it works as expected. But the question arises as to why we want to group it. We want to group it to save it to the filesystem or do some further operations, such as concatenating all the amounts.

We can see that our input is not a normal distribution, since almost all the transactions are for the userId = "A". Because of that, we have a key that is skewed. This means that one key has the majority of the data in it and that the other keys have a lower amount of data. When we use groupBy in Spark, it takes all the elements that have the same grouping, which in this example is userId, and sends those values to exactly the same executors.

For example, if our executors have 5 GB of memory and we have a really big dataset that has hundreds of gigabytes and one key has 90 percent of data, it means that everything will go to one executor and the rest of the executors will take a minority of the data. So, the data will not be normally distributed and, because of the non-uniform distribution, processing will not be as efficient as possible.

So, when we use the groupBy key, we must first answer the question of why we want to group it. Maybe we can filter it or aggregate it at the lower level before groupBy and then we will only group the results, or maybe we don't group at all. We will be investigating how to solve that problem with Spark API in the following sections.

Using the reduce and reduceByKey methods to calculate the results

In this section, we will use the `reduce` and `reduceBykey` functions to calculate our results and understand the behavior of `reduce`. We will then compare the `reduce` and `reduceBykey` functions to check which of the functions should be used in a particular use case.

We will first focus on the `reduce` API. First, we need to create an input of `UserTransaction`. We have the user transaction A with amount 10, B with amount 1, and A with amount 101. Let's say that we want to find out the global maximum. We are not interested in the data for the specific key, but in the global data. We want to scan it, take the maximum, and return it, as shown in the following example:

```
test("should use reduce API") {
    //given
    val input = spark.makeRDD(List(
    UserTransaction("A", 10),
    UserTransaction("B", 1),
    UserTransaction("A", 101)
    ))
```

So, this is the reduced use case. Now, let's see how we can implement it, as per the following example:

```
//when
val result = input
    .map(_.amount)
    .reduce((a, b) => if (a > b) a else b)

//then
assert(result == 101)
}
```

For the `input`, we need to first map the field that we're interested in. In this case, we are interested in `amount`. We will take `amount` and then take the maximum value.

In the preceding code example, `reduce` has two parameters, a and b. One parameter will be the current maximum in the specific Lambda that we are passing, and the second one will be our actual value, which we are investigating now. If the value was higher than the maximum state until now, we will return a; if not, it will return b. We will go through all the elements and, at the end, the result will be just one long number.

```
"C:\Program Files\Java\jdk-12\bin\java.exe" "-javaagent:C:\Program
Files\JetBrains\IntelliJ IDEA 2018.3.5\lib\idea_rt.jar=50894:C:\Program
Files\JetBrains\IntelliJ IDEA 2018.3.5\bin" -Dfile.encoding=UTF-8 -
classpath C:\Users\Sneha\IdeaProjects\Chapter07\out\production\Chapter07
com.company.Main

Process finished with exit code 0
```

Now, let's consider a different situation. We want to find the maximum transaction amount, but this time we want to do it according to users. We not only want to find out the maximum transaction for user A but also for user B, but we want those things to be independent. So, for every key that is the same, we want to take only the maximum value from our data, as shown in the following example:

```
test("should use reduceByKey API") {
    //given
    val input = spark.makeRDD(
    List(
        UserTransaction("A", 10),
        UserTransaction("B", 1),
        UserTransaction("A", 101)
    )
)
```

To achieve this, `reduce` is not a good choice because it will go through all of the values and give us the global maximum. We have key operations in Spark but, first, we want to do it for a specific group of elements. We need to use `keyBy` to tell Spark which ID should be taken as the unique one and it will execute the `reduce` function only within the specific key. So, we use `keyBy(_.userId)` and then we get the `reducedByKey` function. The `reduceByKey` function is similar to `reduce` but it works key-wise so, inside the Lambda, we'll only get values for a specific key, as shown in the following example:

```
    //when
    val result = input
      .keyBy(_.userId)
      .reduceByKey((firstTransaction, secondTransaction) =>
        TransactionChecker.higherTransactionAmount(firstTransaction,
secondTransaction))
      .collect()
      .toList
```

By doing this, we get the first transaction and then the second one. The first one will be a current maximum and the second one will be the transaction that we are investigating right now. We will create a helper function that is taking those transactions and call it higherTransactionAmount.

The higherTransactionAmount function is used in taking the firstTransaction and secondTransaction. Please note that for the UserTransaction type, we need to pass that type. It also needs to return UserTransaction that we cannot return a different type.

If you are using the reduceByKey method from Spark, we need to return the same type as that of the input arguments. If firstTransaction.amount is higher than secondTransaction.amount, we will just return the firstTransaction since we are returning the secondTransaction, so transaction objects not the total amount. This is shown in the following example:

```
object TransactionChecker {
    def higherTransactionAmount(firstTransaction: UserTransaction,
secondTransaction: UserTransaction): UserTransaction = {
        if (firstTransaction.amount > secondTransaction.amount)
firstTransaction else     secondTransaction
    }
}
```

Now, we will collect, add, and test the transaction. After our test, we have the output where, for the key B, we should get transaction ("B", 1) and, for the key A, transaction ("A", 101). There will be no transaction ("A", 10) because we filtered it out, but we can see that for every key, we are able to find out the maximums. This is shown in the following example:

```
    //then
    result should contain theSameElementsAs
      List(("B", UserTransaction("B", 1)), ("A", UserTransaction("A",
101)))
  }

}
```

We can see that the test passed and everything is as expected, as shown in the following output:

```
"C:\Program Files\Java\jdk-12\bin\java.exe" "-javaagent:C:\Program
Files\JetBrains\IntelliJ IDEA 2018.3.5\lib\idea_rt.jar=50909:C:\Program
Files\JetBrains\IntelliJ IDEA 2018.3.5\bin" -Dfile.encoding=UTF-8 -
classpath C:\Users\Sneha\IdeaProjects\Chapter07\out\production\Chapter07
com.company.Main

Process finished with exit code 0
```

In the next section, we will perform actions that trigger the computations of our data.

Performing actions that trigger computations

Spark has a lot more actions that issue DAG, and we should be aware of all of them because they are very important. In this section, we'll understand what can be an action in Spark, do a walk-through of actions, and test those actions if they behave as expected.

The first action we covered is `collect`. We also covered two actions besides that—we covered both `reduce` and `reduceByKey` in the previous section. Both methods are actions because they return a single result.

First, we will create the `input` of our transactions and then apply some transformations just for testing purposes. We will take only the user that contains A, using `keyBy_.userId`, and then take only the amount of the required transaction, as shown in the following example:

```
test("should trigger computations using actions") {
    //given
    val input = spark.makeRDD(
    List(
        UserTransaction(userId = "A", amount = 1001),
        UserTransaction(userId = "A", amount = 100),
        UserTransaction(userId = "A", amount = 102),
        UserTransaction(userId = "A", amount = 1),
        UserTransaction(userId = "B", amount = 13)))

//when apply transformation
 val rdd = input
    .filter(_.userId.contains("A"))
    .keyBy(_.userId)
    .map(_._2.amount)
```

The first action that we are already aware of is `rdd.collect().toList`. The next one is `count()`, which needs to take all of the values and calculate how many values are inside the `rdd`. There is no way to execute `count()` without triggering the transformation. Also, there are different methods in Spark, such as `countApprox`, `countApproxDistinct`, `countByValue`, and `countByValueApprox`. The following example shows us the code for `rdd.collect().toList`:

```
//then
  println(rdd.collect().toList)
  println(rdd.count()) //and all count*
```

If we have a huge dataset and the approximate counter is enough, you can use `countApprox` as it will be a lot faster. We then use `rdd.first()`, but this option is a bit different because it only needs to take the first element. Sometimes, if you want to take the first element and execute everything inside our DAG, we need to be focus on that and check it in the following way:

```
  println(rdd.first())
```

Also, on the `rdd`, we have `foreach()`, which is a for loop to which we can pass any function. A Scala function or a Java function is assumed to be Lambda, but to execute elements of our result `rdd`, DAG needs to be calculated because from here onwards, it is an action. Another variant of the `foreach()` method is `foreachPartition()`, which takes every partition and returns an iterator for the partition. Inside that, we have an iterator to carry our iterations again and then print our elements. We also have our `max()` and `min()` methods and, as expected, `max()` is taking the maximum value and `min()` is taking the minimum value. But these methods are taking the implicit ordering.

If we have an `rdd` of a simple primitive type, like `Long`, we don't need to pass it here. But if we do not use `map()`, we need to define the ordering for the `UserTransaction` for Spark to find out which element is `max` and which element is `min`. These two things need to execute the DAG and so they are classed as actions, as shown in the following example:

```
  rdd.foreach(println(_))
  rdd.foreachPartition(t => t.foreach(println(_)))
  println(rdd.max())
  println(rdd.min())
```

We then have `takeOrdered()`, which is a more time-consuming operation than `first()` because `first()` takes a random element. `takeOrdered()` needs to execute DAG and sort everything. When everything is sorted, only then does it take the top element.

In our example, we are taking num = 1. But sometimes, for testing or monitoring purposes, we need to take only the sample of the data. To take a sample, we use the takeSample() method and pass a number of elements, as shown in the following code:

```
println(rdd.takeOrdered(1).toList)
println(rdd.takeSample(false, 2).toList)
 }
}
```

Now, let's start the test and see the output of implementing the previous actions, as shown in the following screenshot:

```
List(1001, 100, 102 ,1)
4
1001
1001
100
102
1
```

The first action returns all values. The second actions return 4 as a count. We will consider the first element, 1001, but this is a random value and it is not ordered. We will then print all the elements in the loop, as shown in the following output:

```
102
1
1001
1
List(1)
List(100, 1)
```

We then get max and min values like 1001 and 1, which are similar to first(). After that, we get an ordered list, List(1), and sample List(100, 1), which is random. So, in the sample, we get random values from input data and applied transformations.

In the next section, we will learn how to reuse the rdd for different actions.

Reusing the same rdd for different actions

In this section, we will reuse the same rdd for different actions. First, we will minimize the execution time by reusing the rdd. We will then look at caching and a performance test for our code.

The following example is the test from the preceding section but a bit modified, as here we take `start` by `currentTimeMillis()` and the `result`. So, we are just measuring the `result` of all actions that are executed:

```
//then every call to action means that we are going up to the RDD chain
//if we are loading data from external file-system (I.E.: HDFS), every
action means
//that we need to load it from FS.
    val start = System.currentTimeMillis()
    println(rdd.collect().toList)
    println(rdd.count())
    println(rdd.first())
    rdd.foreach(println(_))
    rdd.foreachPartition(t => t.foreach(println(_)))
    println(rdd.max())
    println(rdd.min())
    println(rdd.takeOrdered(1).toList)
    println(rdd.takeSample(false, 2).toList)
    val result = System.currentTimeMillis() - start

    println(s"time taken (no-cache): $result")

}
```

If someone doesn't know Spark very well, they will assume that all actions are cleverly executed. We know that every action count means that we are going up to the `rdd` in the chain, which means we are going to all transformations to load data. In the production system, loading data will be from an external PI system such as HDFS. This means that every action causes the call to the filesystem, which retrieves all data and then applies transformations, as shown in the following example:

```
//when apply transformation
val rdd = input
    .filter(_.userId.contains("A"))
    .keyBy(_.userId)
    .map(_._2.amount)
```

This is a very expensive operation as every action is very costly. When we start this test, we can see that the time taken without caching will take `632` milliseconds, as shown in the following output:

```
List(1)
List(100, 1)
time taken (no-cache): 632
Process finished with exit code 0
```

Let's compare this with the caching use. Our test, at first glance, looks very similar, but this is not the same because you are issuing `cache()` and we are returning `rdd`. So, `rdd` will be already cached and every subsequent call to the `rdd` will go through the `cache`, as shown in the following example:

```
//when apply transformation
val rdd = input
    .filter(_.userId.contains("A"))
    .keyBy(_.userId)
    .map(_._2.amount)
    .cache()
```

The first action will execute DAG, save the data into our cache, and then the subsequent actions will just retrieve the specific things according to the method that was called from memory. There will be no HDFS lookup, so let's start this test, as per the following example, and see how long it takes:

```
//then every call to action means that we are going up to the RDD chain
//if we are loading data from external file-system (I.E.: HDFS), every
action means
//that we need to load it from FS.
    val start = System.currentTimeMillis()
    println(rdd.collect().toList)
    println(rdd.count())
    println(rdd.first())
    rdd.foreach(println(_))
    rdd.foreachPartition(t => t.foreach(println(_)))
    println(rdd.max())
    println(rdd.min())
    println(rdd.takeOrdered(1).toList)
    println(rdd.takeSample(false, 2).toList)
    val result = System.currentTimeMillis() - start

    println(s"time taken(cache): $result")


    }
  }
```

The first output will be as follows:

```
List(1)
List(100, 102)
time taken (no-cache): 585
List(1001, 100, 102, 1)
4
```

The second output will be as follows:

```
1
List(1)
List(102, 1)
time taken(cache): 336
Process finished with exit code 0
```

Without cache, the value is 585 milliseconds and with cache, the value is 336. The difference is not much as we are just creating data in tests. However, in real production systems, this will be a big difference because we need to look up data from external filesystems.

Summary

So, let's sum up this chapter. Firstly, we used Spark transformations to defer computation to a later time, and then we learned which transformations should be avoided. Next, we looked at how to use reduceByKey and reduce to calculate our result globally and per specific key. After that, we performed actions that triggered computations then learned that every action means a call to the loading data. To alleviate that problem, we learned how to reduce the same rdd for different actions.

In the next chapter, we'll be looking at the immutable design of the Spark engine.

8
Immutable Design

In this chapter, we will look at the immutable design of Apache Spark. We will delve into the Spark RDD's parent/child chain and use RDD in an immutable way. We will then use DataFrame operations for transformations to discuss immutability in a highly concurrent environment. By the end of this chapter, we will use the Dataset API in an immutable way.

In this chapter, we will cover the following topics:

- Delving into the Spark RDD's parent/child chain
- Using RDD in an immutable way
- Using DataFrame operations to transform
- Immutability in the highly concurrent environment
- Using the Dataset API in an immutable way

Delving into the Spark RDD's parent/child chain

In this section, we will try to implement our own RDD that inherits the parent properties of RDD.

We will go through the following topics:

- Extending an RDD
- Chaining a new RDD with the parent
- Testing our custom RDD

Extending an RDD

This is a simple test that has a lot of hidden complexity. Let's start by creating a list of the record, as shown in the following code block:

```
class InheritanceRdd extends FunSuite {
  val spark: SparkContext = SparkSession
    .builder().master("local[2]").getOrCreate().sparkContext

  test("use extended RDD") {
    //given
    val rdd = spark.makeRDD(List(Record(1, "d1")))
```

The Record is just a case class that has an amount and description, so the amount is 1 and d1 is the description.

We then created MultipledRDD and passed rdd to it, and then set the multiplier equal to 10, as shown in the following code:

```
val extendedRdd = new MultipliedRDD(rdd, 10)
```

We are passing the parent RDD because it has data that was loaded in another RDD. In this way, we build the inheritance chain of two RDD's.

Chaining a new RDD with the parent

We first created a multiple RDD class. In the MultipliedRDD class, we have two things that pass the parameters:

- A brief RDD of the record, that is, RDD[Record]
- A multiplier, that is, Double

In our case, there could be a chain of multiple RDD's, which means that there could be multiple RDD's inside our RDD. So, this is not always the parent of all the directed acyclic graphs. We are just extending the RDD of the type record and so we need to pass the RDD that is extended.

RDD has a lot of methods and we can override any method we want. However, this time, we are going with the `compute` method, where we will override the compute method to calculate the multiplier. Here, we get a `Partition` split and `TaskContext`. These are passed by this part execution engine to our method, so we don't need to worry about this. However, we need to return the iterator of the exact same type as the type that we pass through the RDD class in the inheritance chain. This will be an iterator of the record.

We then execute the first parent logic, where the first parent is just taking that first RDD in our chain. The type here is `Record`, and we are taking an `iterator` of `split` and `context`, where the `split` is just a partition that will be executed. We know that the Spark RDD is partitioned by the partitioner, but, here, we are just getting the specific partition that we need to split. So, the iterator is taking the partition and task context, and so it knows which values should be returned from that iterative method. For every record in that iterator, which is a `salesRecord`, like `amount` and `description`, we are multiplying the `amount` by the `multiplier` that was passed to the constructor to get our `Double`.

By doing this, we have multiplied our amount by the multiplier, and we can then return the new record which has the new amount. So, we now have an amount of the old record multiplied by our `multiplier` and the description of the `salesRecord`. For the second filter, what we need to `override` is `getPartitions`, as we want to keep the partitioning of the parent RDD. If the previous RDD has 100 partitions, for example, we also want our `MultipledRDD` to have 100 partitions. So, we want to retain that information about partitions rather than losing it. For the same reason, we are just proxying it to the `firstParent`. The `firstParent` of the RDD will then just take the previous partitions from that specific RDD.

In this way, we have created a new `multipliedRDD`, which passes the parent and multiplier. For our `extendedRDD`, we need to `collect` it and call `toList`, and our list should have `10` and `d1`, as shown in the following example:

```
extendedRdd.collect().toList should contain theSameElementsAs List(
Record(10, "d1")
)
}
}
```

 Compute was executed automatically when we created the new RDD, and so it is always executed without the explicit method call.

Testing our custom RDD

Let's start this test to check if this has created our RDD. By doing this, we can extend our parent RDD and add behavior to our RDD. This is shown in the following screenshot:

```
"C:\Program Files\Java\jdk-12\bin\java.exe" "-javaagent:C:\Program
Files\JetBrains\IntelliJ IDEA 2018.3.5\lib\idea_rt.jar=51687:C:\Program
Files\JetBrains\IntelliJ IDEA 2018.3.5\bin" -Dfile.encoding=UTF-8 -
classpath C:\Users\Sneha\IdeaProjects\Chapter07\out\production\Chapter07
com.company.Main

Process finished with exit code 0
```

In the next section, we'll be using RDD in an immutable way.

Using RDD in an immutable way

Now that we know how to create a chain of execution using RDD inheritance, let's learn how to use RDD in an immutable way.

In this section, we will go through the following topics:

- Understating DAG immutability
- Creating two leaves from the one root RDD
- Examining results from both leaves

Let's first understand directed acyclic graph immutability and what it gives us. We will then be creating two leaves from one node RDD, and checking if both leaves are behaving totally independently if we create a transformation on one of the leaf RDD's. We will then examine results from both leaves of our current RDD and check if any transformation on any leaf does not change or impact the root RDD. It is imperative to work like this because we have found that we will not be able to create yet another leaf from the root RDD, because the root RDD will be changed, which means it will be mutable. To overcome this, the Spark designers created an immutable RDD for us.

There is a simple test to show that the RDD should be immutable. First, we will create an RDD from 0 to 5, which is added to a sequence from the Scala branch. to is taking the Int, and the first parameter is an implicit one, which is from the Scala package, as shown in the following example:

```
class ImmutableRDD extends FunSuite {
    val spark: SparkContext = SparkSession
        .builder().master("local[2]").getOrCreate().sparkContext
```

```
test("RDD should be immutable") {
    //given
    val data = spark.makeRDD(0 to 5)
```

Once we have our RDD data, we can create the first leaf. The first leaf is a result (res) and we are just mapping every element multiplied by 2. Let's create a second leaf, but this time it will be marked by 4, as shown in the following example:

```
//when
val res = data.map(_ * 2)

val leaf2 = data.map(_ * 4)
```

So, we have our root RDD and two leaves. First, we will collect the first leaf and see that the elements in it are 0, 2, 4, 6, 8, 10, so everything here is multiplied by 2, as shown in the following example:

```
//then
res.collect().toList should contain theSameElementsAs List(
    0, 2, 4, 6, 8, 10
)
```

However, even though we have that notification on the res, the data is still exactly the same as it was in the beginning, which is 0, 1, 2, 3, 4, 5, as shown in the following example:

```
data.collect().toList should contain theSameElementsAs List(
    0, 1, 2, 3, 4, 5
    )
  }
}
```

So, everything is immutable, and executing the transformation of * 2 didn't change our data. If we create a test for leaf2, we will collect it and call toList. We will see that it should contain elements like 0, 4, 8, 12, 16, 20, as shown in the following example:

```
leaf2.collect().toList should contain theSameElementsAs List(
  0, 4, 8, 12, 16, 20
  )
```

When we run the test, we will see that every path in our execution, the root, that is, data, or the first leaf and second leaf, behave independently from each other, as shown in the following code output:

```
"C:\Program Files\Java\jdk-12\bin\java.exe" "-javaagent:C:\Program
Files\JetBrains\IntelliJ IDEA 2018.3.5\lib\idea_rt.jar=51704:C:\Program
Files\JetBrains\IntelliJ IDEA 2018.3.5\bin" -Dfile.encoding=UTF-8 -
classpath C:\Users\Sneha\IdeaProjects\Chapter07\out\production\Chapter07
com.company.Main

Process finished with exit code 0
```

Every mutation is different; we can see that the test passed, which shows us that our RDD is immutable.

Using DataFrame operations to transform

The data from the API has an RDD underneath it, and so there is no way that the DataFrame could be mutable. In DataFrame, the immutability is even better because we can add and subtract columns from it dynamically, without changing the source dataset.

In this section, we will cover the following topics:

- Understanding DataFrame immutability
- Creating two leaves from the one root DataFrame
- Adding a new column by issuing transformation

We will start by using data from operations to transform our DataFrame. First, we need to understand DataFrame immutability and then we will create two leaves, but this time from the one root DataFrame. We will then issue a transformation that is a bit different than the RDD. This will add a new column to our resulting DataFrame because we are manipulating it this way in a DataFrame. If we want to map data, then we need to take data from the first column, transform it, and save it to another column, and then we'll have two columns. If we are no longer interested, we can drop the first column, but the result will be yet another DataFrame.

So, we'll have the first DataFrame with one column, the second one with result and source, and the third one with only one result. Let's look at the code for this section.

We will be creating a DataFrame, so we need to call the `toDF()` method. We are creating the `UserData` with "a" as "1", "b" as "2", and "d" as "200". The `UserData` has `userID` and `data`, two fields that are both `String`, as shown in the following example:

```
test("Should use immutable DF API") {
 import spark.sqlContext.implicits._
 //given
 val userData =
 spark.sparkContext.makeRDD(List(
 UserData("a", "1"),
 UserData("b", "2"),
 UserData("d", "200")
 )).toDF()
```

It is important to create an RDD using a case class in tests because, when we are called to the DataFrame, this part will infer the schema and name columns accordingly. The following code follows an example of this, where we are filtering only a `userID` column from the `userData` that is in "a":

```
//when
    val res = userData.filter(userData("userId").isin("a"))
```

Our result should have only one record and so we are dropping two columns, but still, the `userData` source that we created will have 3 rows. So, modifying it by filtering created yet another DataFrame that we call the `res` without modifying the input `userData`, as shown in the following example:

```
        assert(res.count() == 1)
        assert(userData.count() == 3)

    }
}
```

So, let's start this test and see how immutable data from API behaves, as shown in the following screenshot:

```
"C:\Program Files\Java\jdk-12\bin\java.exe" "-javaagent:C:\Program
Files\JetBrains\IntelliJ IDEA 2018.3.5\lib\idea_rt.jar=51713:C:\Program
Files\JetBrains\IntelliJ IDEA 2018.3.5\bin" -Dfile.encoding=UTF-8 -
classpath C:\Users\Sneha\IdeaProjects\Chapter07\out\production\Chapter07
com.company.Main

Process finished with exit code 0
```

As we can see, our test passes, and, from the result (`res`), we know that our parent was not modified. So, for example, if we want to map something on `res.map()`, we can map the `userData` column, as shown in the following example:

```
res.map(a => a.getString("userId") + "can")
```

Another leaf will have an additional column without changing the `userId` source code, so that was the immutability of DataFrame.

Immutability in the highly concurrent environment

We saw how immutability affects the creation and design of programs, so now we will understand how it is useful.

In this section, we will cover the following topics:

- The cons of mutable collections
- Creating two threads that simultaneously modify a mutable collection
- Reasoning about a concurrent program

Let's first understand the cause of mutable collections. To do this, we will be creating two threads that simultaneously modify the mutable collection. We will be using this code for our test. First, we will create a `ListBuffer` that is a mutable list. Then, we can add and delete links without creating another list for any modification. We can then create an `Executors` service with two threads. We need two threads to start simultaneously to modify the state. Later, we will use a `CountDownLatch` construct from `Java.util.concurrent:`. This is shown in the following example:

```
import java.util.concurrent.{CountDownLatch, Executors}
import org.scalatest.FunSuite
import scala.collection.mutable.ListBuffer
class MultithreadedImmutabilityTest extends FunSuite {

test("warning: race condition with mutability") {
//given
var listMutable = new ListBuffer[String]()
val executors = Executors.newFixedThreadPool(2)
val latch = new CountDownLatch(2)
```

The `CountDownLatch` is a construct that helps us to stop threads from processing until we request them to. We need to wait with our logic until both threads start executing. We then submit a `Runnable` to the `executors` and our `run()` method does the `countDown()` by signaling when it is ready for action and appends `"A"` to `listMutable`, as shown in the following example:

```
//when
executors.submit(new Runnable {
    override def run(): Unit = {
        latch.countDown()
        listMutable += "A"
    }
})
```

Then, another thread starts, and also uses `countDown` by signaling that it is ready to start. But first, it checks whether the list contains `"A"` and, if not, it appends that `"A"`, as shown in the following example:

```
executors.submit(new Runnable {
    override def run(): Unit = {
        latch.countDown()
        if(!listMutable.contains("A")) {
            listMutable += "A"
        }
    }
})
```

We then use `await()` to wait until `countDown` is issued and, when it is issued, we are able to progress with the verification of our program, as shown in the following example:

```
        latch.await()
```

`listMutable` contains `"A"` or it can have `"A"`, `"A"`. `listMutable` checks if the list contains `"A"` and, if not, it will not add that element, as shown in the following example:

```
    //then
    //listMutable can have ("A") or ("A","A")
    }
}
```

But there is a race condition here. There could be a possibility that, after the check `if(!listMutable.contains("A"))`, the `run()` thread will add the `"A"` element to the list. But we are inside `if`, so we will add another `"A"` by/using `listMutable += "A"`. Because of the mutability of the state and the fact that it was modified via another thread, we can have `"A"` or `"A"`, `"A"`.

We need to be careful while using mutable state since we cannot have such a corrupted state. To alleviate this problem, we can use `java.util` collections and synchronized lists on it.

But if we have the synchronized block, then our program will be very slow because we will need to coordinate access to that exclusively. We can also employ `lock` from the `java.util.concurrent.locks` package. We can use an implementation, like `ReadLock` or `WriteLock`. In the following example, we will use `WriteLock`:

```
val lock = new WriteLock()
```

We also need to `lock` our `lock()` and only then proceed, as shown in the following example:

```
lock.lock()
```

Later, we can use `unlock()`. However, we should also do this in the second thread so that our list only has one element, as shown in the following example:

```
lock.unlock()
```

The output is as follows:

Locking is a very hard and expensive operation, and so immutability is key to performance programs.

Using the Dataset API in an immutable way

In this section, we will use the Dataset API in an immutable way. We will cover the following topics:

- Dataset immutability
- Creating two leaves from the one root dataset
- Adding a new column by issuing transformation

The test case for the dataset is quite similar, but we need to do a `toDS()` for our data to be type safe. The type of dataset is `userData`, as shown in the following example:

```
import com.tomekl007.UserData
import org.apache.spark.sql.SparkSession
import org.scalatest.FunSuite

class ImmutableDataSet extends FunSuite {
  val spark: SparkSession = SparkSession
  .builder().master("local[2]").getOrCreate()

test("Should use immutable DF API") {
  import spark.sqlContext.implicits._
  //given
  val userData =
  spark.sparkContext.makeRDD(List(
  UserData("a", "1"),
  UserData("b", "2"),
  UserData("d", "200")
  )).toDF()
```

Now, we will issue a filter of `userData` and specify `isin`, as shown in the following example:

```
//when
  val res = userData.filter(userData("userId").isin("a"))
```

It will return the result (`res`), which is a leaf with our 1 element. `userData` will still have 3 elements because of this apparent root. Let's execute this program, as shown in the following example:

```
assert(res.count() == 1)
  assert(userData.count() == 3)

}
}
```

We can see our test passed, which means that the dataset is also an immutable abstraction on top of the DataFrame, and employs the same characteristics. `userData` has a something very useful known as a typeset, and, if you use the `show()` method, it will infer the schema and know that the `"a"` field is a string or another type, as shown in the following example:

```
userData.show()
```

The output will be as follows:

```
+------+----+
|userId|data|
|----- |----|
|     a|   1|
|     b|   2|
|     d| 200|
+------|----+
```

In the preceding output, we have both `userID` and `data` fields.

Summary

In this chapter, we delved into the Spark RDD parent-child chain and created a multiplier RDD that was able to calculate everything based on the parent RDD, and also based on the partitioning scheme on the parent. We used RDD in an immutable way. We saw that the modification of the leaf that was created from the parent didn't modify the part. We also learned a better abstraction, that is, a DataFrame, so we learned that we can employ transformation there. However, every transformation is just adding to another column—it is not modifying anything in place. Next, we just set immutability in a highly concurrent environment. We saw how the mutable state is bad when accessing multiple threads. Finally, we saw that the Dataset API is also created in an immutable type of way and that we can leverage those things here.

In the next chapter, we'll look at how to avoid shuffle and reduce personal expense.

9
Avoiding Shuffle and Reducing Operational Expenses

In this chapter, we will learn how to avoid shuffle and reduce the operational expense of our jobs, along with detecting a shuffle in a process. We will then test operations that cause a shuffle in Apache Spark to find out when we should be very careful and which operations we should avoid. Next, we will learn how to change the design of jobs with wide dependencies. After that, we will be using the keyBy() operations to reduce shuffle and, in the last section of this chapter, we'll see how we can use custom partitioning to reduce the shuffle of our data.

In this chapter, we will cover the following topics:

- Detecting a shuffle in a process
- Testing operations that cause a shuffle in Apache Spark
- Changing the design of jobs with wide dependencies
- Using keyBy() operations to reduce shuffle
- Using the custom partitioner to reduce shuffle

Detecting a shuffle in a process

In this section, we will learn how to detect a shuffle in a process.

In this section, we will cover the following topics:

- Loading randomly partitioned data
- Issuing repartition using a meaningful partition key
- Understanding how shuffle occurs by explaining a query

We will load randomly partitioned data to see how and where the data is loaded. Next, we will issue a partition using a meaningful partition key. We will then repartition data to the proper executors using the deterministic and meaningful key. In the end, we will explain our queries by using the `explain()` method and understand the shuffle. Here, we have a very simple test.

We will create a DataFrame with some data. For example, we created an `InputRecord` with some random UID and `user_1`, and another input with random ID in `user_1`, and the last record for `user_2`. Let's imagine that this data is loaded through the external data system. The data can be loaded from HDFS or from a database, such as Cassandra or NoSQL:

```
class DetectingShuffle extends FunSuite {
  val spark: SparkSession =
SparkSession.builder().master("local[2]").getOrCreate()

  test("should explain plan showing logical and physical with UDF and DF")
{
    //given
    import spark.sqlContext.implicits._
    val df = spark.sparkContext.makeRDD(List(
      InputRecord("1234-3456-1235-1234", "user_1"),
      InputRecord("1123-3456-1235-1234", "user_1"),
      InputRecord("1123-3456-1235-9999", "user_2")
    )).toDF()
```

In the loaded data, there is no predefined or meaningful partitioning of our data, which means that the input record number 1 can end up in the executor first, and record number 2 can end up in the executor second. So, even though the data is from the same user, it is likely that we'll be executing operations for the specific user.

As discussed in the previous chapter, Chapter 8, *Immutable Design*, we used the `reducebyKey()` method that was taking the user ID or specific ID to reduce all values for the specific key. This is a very common operation but with some random partitioning. It is good practice to `repartition` the data using a meaningful key.

While using `userID`, we will use `repartition` in a way that the result will record the data that has the same user ID. So `user_1`, for example, will end up on the first executor:

```
//when
    val q = df.repartition(df("userId"))
```

The first executor will have all the data for `userID`.
If `InputRecord("1234-3456-1235-1234", "user_1")` is on executor 1
and `InputRecord("1123-3456-1235-1234", "user_1")` is on executor 2, after
partitioning the data from executor 2, we will need to send it to executor 1, because it is a
parent for this partition key. This causes a shuffle. A shuffle is caused by loading data that
is not meaningfully partitioned, or not partitioned at all. We need to process our data so
that we can perform operations on a specific key.

We can `repartition` the data further, but it should be done at the beginning of our chain.
Let's start the test to explain our query:

```
q.explain(true)
```

We are repartitioning the `userID` expression in a logical plan, but when we check the
physical plan, it shows that a hash partition is used and that we will be hashing on
the `userID` value. So, we scan all the RDDs and all the keys that have the same hash and
are sent to the same executor to achieve our goal:

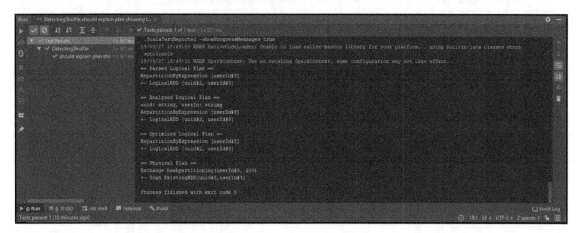

In the next section, we'll test operations that cause a shuffle in Apache Spark.

Testing operations that cause a shuffle in Apache Spark

In this section, we will test the operations that cause a shuffle in Apache Spark. We will cover the following topics:

- Using join for two DataFrames
- Using two DataFrames that are partitioned differently
- Testing a join that causes a shuffle

A join is a specific operation that causes shuffle, and we will use it to join our two DataFrames. We will first check whether it causes shuffle and then we will check how to avoid it. To understand this, we will use two DataFrames that are partitioned differently and check the operation of joining two datasets or DataFrames that are not partitioned or partitioned randomly. It will cause shuffle because there is no way to join two datasets with the same partition key if they are on different physical machines.

Before we join the dataset, we need to send them to the same physical machine. We will be using the following test.

We need to create `UserData`, which is a case class that we have seen already. It has the user ID and data. We have user IDs, that is, `user_1`, `user_2`, and `user_4`:

```
test("example of operation that is causing shuffle") {
    import spark.sqlContext.implicits._
    val userData =
    spark.sparkContext.makeRDD(List(
        UserData("user_1", "1"),
        UserData("user_2", "2"),
        UserData("user_4", "200")
    )).toDS()
```

We then create some transactional data similar to a user ID (`user_1`, `user_2`, and `user_3`):

```
val transactionData =
    spark.sparkContext.makeRDD(List(
        UserTransaction("user_1", 100),
        UserTransaction("user_2", 300),
        UserTransaction("user_3", 1300)
    )).toDS()
```

We use the `joinWith` transaction on `UserData` by using the `userID` column from
`UserData` and `transactionData`. Since we have issued an `inner` join, the result has two
elements because there is a join between the record and the transaction, that is, `UserData`,
and `UserTransaction`. However, `UserData` has no transaction and `Usertransaction`
has no user data:

```
//shuffle: userData can stay on the current executors, but data from
//transactionData needs to be send to those executors according to
joinColumn
//causing shuffle
//when
val res: Dataset[(UserData, UserTransaction)]
= userData.joinWith(transactionData, userData("userId") ===
transactionData("userId"), "inner")
```

When we were joining the data, the data was not partitioned because this was some
random data for Spark. It was unable to know that the user ID column is the partition key,
as it cannot guess this. Since it is not pre-partitioned, to join the data from two datasets, will
need to send data from the user ID to the executor. Hence, there will be a lot of data
shuffling from the executor, which is because the data is not partitioned.

Let's explain the query, perform an assert, and show the results by starting the test:

```
//then
 res.show()
 assert(res.count() == 2)
 }
}
```

We can see our result as follows:

```
+-------------+---------------+
|          _1 |            _2|
+------------  +--------------+
+ [user_1,1]  | [user_1,100]|
| [user_2,2]  | [user_2,300]|
+-------------+--------------+
```

We have `[user_1,1]` and `[user_1,100]`, which is `userID` and `userTransaction`. It
appears that the join worked properly, but let's look at that physical parameter. We
had `SortMergeJoin` use `userID` for the first dataset and the second one, and then we
used `Sort` and `hashPartitioning`.

In the previous section, *Detecting a shuffle in a process*, we used the `partition` method, which uses `hashPartitioning` underneath. Although we are using `join`, we still need to use hash partitioning because our data is not properly partitioned. So, we need to partition the first dataset as there will be a lot of shuffling, and then we need to do exactly the same thing for the second DataFrame. Again, the shuffling will be done twice, and once that data is partitioned on the joined field, the join could be local to the executor.

There will be an assertion of records after executing the physical plan, stating that the `userID` user data one is on the same executor as that of user transaction `userID` one. Without `hashPartitioning`, there is no guarantee and hence we need to do the partitioning.

In the next section, we'll learn how to change the design of jobs with wide dependencies, so we will see how to avoid unnecessary shuffling when performing a join on two datasets.

Changing the design of jobs with wide dependencies

In this section, we will change the job that was performing the `join` on non-partitioned data. We'll be changing the design of jobs with wide dependencies.

In this section, we will cover the following topics:

- Repartitioning DataFrames using a common partition key
- Understanding a join with pre-partitioned data
- Understanding that we avoided shuffle

We will be using the `repartition` method on the DataFrame using a common partition key. We saw that when issuing a join, repartitioning happens underneath. But often, when using Spark, we want to execute multiple operations on the DataFrame. So, when we perform the join with other datasets, `hashPartitioning` will need to be executed once again. If we do the partition at the beginning when the data is loaded, we will avoid partitioning again.

Here, we have our example test case, with the data we used previously in the *Testing operations that cause a shuffle in Apache Spark* section. We have `UserData` with three records for user ID – `user_1`, `user_2`, and `user_4` – and the `UserTransaction` data with the user ID – that is, `user_1`, `user_2`, `user_3`:

```
test("example of operation that is causing shuffle") {
    import spark.sqlContext.implicits._
    val userData =
        spark.sparkContext.makeRDD(List(
            UserData("user_1", "1"),
            UserData("user_2", "2"),
            UserData("user_4", "200")
        )).toDS()
```

Then, we need to `repartition` the data, which is the first very important thing to do. We are repartitioning our `userData` using the `userId` column:

```
val repartitionedUserData = userData.repartition(userData("userId"))
```

Then, we will repartition our data using the `userId` column, this time for `transactionData`:

```
val repartitionedTransactionData =
transactionData.repartition(transactionData("userId"))
```

Once we have our data repartitioned, we have the assurance that any data that has the same partition key – in this example, it's `userId` – will land on the same executor. Because of that, our repartitioned data will not have the shuffle, and the joins will be faster. In the end, we are able to join, but this time we are joining the pre-partitioned data:

```
//when
//data is already partitioned using join-column. Don't need to shuffle
val res: Dataset[(UserData, UserTransaction)]
= repartitionedUserData.joinWith(repartitionedTransactionData,
userData("userId") === transactionData("userId"), "inner")
```

We can show our results using the following code:

```
//then
res.show()
assert(res.count() == 2)
 }
}
```

The output is shown in the following screenshot:

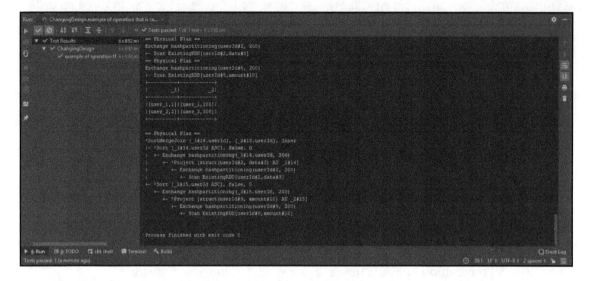

In the preceding screenshot, we have our physical plans for user ID and transactions. We perform a hash partitioning on the user ID column of the user ID data and also on the transaction data. After joining the data, we can see that the data is proper and that there is a physical plan for the join.

This time, the physical plan is a bit different.

We have a `SortMergeJoin` operation, and we are sorting our data that is already pre-partitioned in the previous step of our execution engine. In this way, our Spark engine will perform the sort-merge join, where we don't need to hash join. It will sort data properly and the join will be faster.

In the next section, we'll be using `keyBy()` operations to reduce shuffle even further.

Using keyBy() operations to reduce shuffle

In this section, we will use `keyBy()` operations to reduce shuffle. We will cover the following topics:

- Loading randomly partitioned data
- Trying to pre-partition data in a meaningful way
- Leveraging the `keyBy()` function

We will load randomly partitioned data, but this time using the RDD API. We will repartition the data in a meaningful way and extract the information that is going on underneath, similar to DataFrame and the Dataset API. We will learn how to leverage the `keyBy()` function to give our data some structure and to cause the pre-partitioning in the RDD API.

Here is the test we will be using in this section. We are creating two random input records. The first record has a random user ID, `user_1`, the second one has a random user ID, `user_1`, and the third one has a random user ID, `user_2`:

```
test("Should use keyBy to distribute traffic properly"){
    //given
    val rdd = spark.sparkContext.makeRDD(List(
        InputRecord("1234-3456-1235-1234", "user_1"),
        InputRecord("1123-3456-1235-1234", "user_1"),
        InputRecord("1123-3456-1235-9999", "user_2")
    ))
```

We will extract what is happening underneath Spark using `rdd.toDebugString`:

```
println(rdd.toDebugString)
```

At this point, our data is spread randomly and the records for the user ID field could be on different executors because the Spark execution engine cannot guess whether `user_1` is a meaningful key for us or whether `1234-3456-1235-1234` is. We know that `1234-3456-1235-1234` is not a meaningful key, and that it is a unique identifier. Using that field as a partition key will give us a random distribution and a lot of shuffling because there is no data locality when you use the unique field as a partition key.

There is no possibility for Spark to know that data for the same user ID will land on the same executor, and that's why we need to use the user ID field, either `user_1`, `user_1`, or `user_2`, when partitioning the data. To achieve that in the RDD API, we can use `keyBy(_.userId)` in our data, but this time it will change the RDD type:

```
val res = rdd.keyBy(_.userId)
```

If we check the RDD type, we'll see that this time, an RDD is not an input record, but it is an RDD of the string and input record. The string is a type of the field that we expected here, and it is `userId`. We will also extract information about the `keyBy()` function by using `toDebugString` on the result:

```
println(res.toDebugString)
```

Once we use `keyBy()`, all the records for the same user ID will land on the same executor. As we have discussed, this can be dangerous because if we have a skew key, it means that we have a key that has very high cardinality, and we can run out of memory. Also, all operations on a result will be key-wise, so we'll be on the pre-partitioned data:

```
res.collect()
```

Let's start this test. The output will be as follows:

We can see that our first debug string is a very simple one, and we have only the collection on the RDD, but the second one is a bit different. We have a `keyBy()` method and we make an RDD underneath it. We have our child RDD and parent RDD from the first section, *Testing operations that cause a shuffle in Apache Spark*, from when we extended the RDD. This a parent-child chain that's issued by the `keyBy()` method.

In the next section, we'll use a custom partitioner to reduce shuffle even further.

Using a custom partitioner to reduce shuffle

In this section, we will use a custom partitioner to reduce shuffle. We will cover the following topics:

- Implementing a custom partitioner
- Using the partitioner with the `partitionBy` method on Spark
- Validating that our data was partitioned properly

We will implement a custom partitioner with our custom logic, which will partition the data. It will inform Spark where each record should land and on which executor. We will be using the `partitionBy` method on Spark. In the end, we will validate that our data was partitioned properly. For the purposes of this test, we are assuming that we have two executors:

```
import com.tomekl007.UserTransaction
import org.apache.spark.sql.SparkSession
```

```
import org.apache.spark.{Partitioner, SparkContext}
import org.scalatest.FunSuite
import org.scalatest.Matchers._

class CustomPartitioner extends FunSuite {
val spark: SparkContext =
SparkSession.builder().master("local[2]").getOrCreate().sparkContext

test("should use custom partitioner") {
//given
val numberOfExecutors = 2
```

Let's assume that we want to split our data evenly into 2 executors and that the instances of data with the same key will land on the same executor. So, our input data is a list of UserTransactions: "a", "b", "a", "b", and "c". The values are not so important, but we need to keep them in mind to test the behavior later. The amount is 100, 101, 202, 1, and 55 for the given UserTransactions:

```
val data = spark
    .parallelize(List(
        UserTransaction("a", 100),
        UserTransaction("b", 101),
        UserTransaction("a", 202),
        UserTransaction("b", 1),
        UserTransaction("c", 55)
```

When we do a keyBy, (_.userId) is passed to our partitioner and so when we issue partitionBy, we need to extend override methods:

```
).keyBy(_.userId)
.partitionBy(new Partitioner {
    override def numPartitions: Int = numberOfExecutors
```

The getPartition method takes a key, which will be the userId. The key will be passed here and the type will be a string:

```
override def getPartition(key: Any): Int = {
    key.hashCode % numberOfExecutors
    }
})
```

The signature of these methods is Any, so we need to override it, and also override the number of partitions.

We then print our two partitions, and `numPartitions` returns the value of 2:

```
println(data.partitions.length)
```

`getPartition` is very simple as it takes the `hashCode`
and `numberOfExecutors` modules. It ensures that the same key will land on the same executor.

We will then map every partition for the respective partition as we get an iterator. Here, we are taking `amount` for a test purpose:

```
//when
val res = data.mapPartitions[Long](iter =>
iter.map(_._2).map(_.amount)
).collect().toList
```

In the end, we assert `55`, `100`, `202`, `101`, and `1`; the order is random, so there is no need to take care of the order:

```
//then
res should contain theSameElementsAs List(55, 100, 202, 101, 1)
}
}
```

If we still want to, we should use a `sortBy` method. Let's start this test and see whether our custom partitioner works as expected. Now, we can start. We have 2 partitions, so it works as expected, as shown in the following screenshot:

Summary

In this chapter, we learned how to detect shuffle in a process. We covered testing operations that cause a shuffle in Apache Spark. We also learned how to employ partitioning in the RDD. It is important to know how to use the API if partitioned data is needed, because RDD is still widely used, so we use the `keyBy` operations to reduce shuffle. We also learned how to use the custom partitioner to reduce shuffle.

In the next chapter, we'll learn how to save data in the correct format using the Spark API.

10
Saving Data in the Correct Format

In the previous chapters, we were focusing on processing and loading data. We learned about transformations, actions, joining, shuffling, and other aspects of Spark.

In this chapter, we will learn how to save data in the correct format and also save data in plain text format using Spark's standard API. We will also leverage JSON as a data format, and learn how to use standard APIs to save JSON. Spark has a CSV format and we will leverage that format as well. We will then learn more advanced schema-based formats, where support is required to import third-party dependencies. Following that, we will use Avro with Spark and learn how to use and save the data in a columnar format known as Parquet. By the end of this chapter, we will have also learned how to retrieve data to validate whether it is stored in the proper way.

In this chapter, we will cover the following topics:

- Saving data in plain text format
- Leveraging JSON as a data format
- Tabular formats – CSV
- Using Avro with Spark
- Columnar formats – Parquet

Saving data in plain text format

In this section, we will learn how to save data in plain text format. The following topics will be covered:

- Saving data in plain text format
- Loading plain text data
- Testing

We will save our data in plain text format and investigate how to save it into the Spark directory. We will then load the plain text data, and then test and save it to check whether we can yield the same results code. This is our `SavePlainText.scala` file:

```scala
package com.tomekl007.chapter_4

import java.io.File

import com.tomekl007.UserTransaction
import org.apache.spark.sql.SparkSession
import org.apache.spark.{Partitioner, SparkContext}
import org.scalatest.{BeforeAndAfterEach, FunSuite}
import org.scalatest.Matchers._

import scala.reflect.io.Path

class SavePlainText extends FunSuite with BeforeAndAfterEach{
    val spark: SparkContext =
SparkSession.builder().master("local[2]").getOrCreate().sparkContext

    private val FileName = "transactions.txt"

    override def afterEach() {
        val path = Path (FileName)
        path.deleteRecursively()
    }

    test("should save and load in plain text") {
        //given
        val rdd = spark.makeRDD(List(UserTransaction("a", 100),
UserTransaction("b", 200)))

        //when
        rdd.coalesce(1).saveAsTextFile(FileName)

        val fromFile = spark.textFile(FileName)
```

```
        fromFile.collect().toList should contain theSameElementsAs List(
            "UserTransaction(a,100)", "UserTransaction(b,200)"
            //note - this is string!
        )
    }
}
```

We will need a `FileName` variable, which, in our case, will be a folder name, and Spark will then create a couple of files underneath:

```
import java.io.File
import com.tomekl007.UserTransaction
import org.apache.spark.sql.SparkSession
import org.apache.spark.{Partitioner, SparkContext}
import org.scalatest.{BeforeAndAfterEach, FunSuite}
import org.scalatest.Matchers._
import scala.reflect.io.Path
class SavePlainText extends FunSuite with BeforeAndAfterEach{
    val spark: SparkContext =
SparkSession.builder().master("local[2]").getOrCreate().sparkContext
    private val FileName = "transactions.txt"
```

We will use `BeforeAndAfterEach` in our test case to clean our directory after every test, which means that the path should be deleted recursively. The whole path is deleted after the test, as it is required to rerun the tests without a failure. We need to comment the following code out for the first run to investigate the structure of the saved text file:

```
//override def afterEach() {
//          val path = Path (FileName)
//          path.deleteRecursively()
//      }

//test("should save and load in plain text") {
```

We will then create an RDD of two transactions, `UserTransaction("a", 100)` and `UserTransaction("b", 200)`:

```
val rdd = spark.makeRDD(List(UserTransaction("a", 100),
UserTransaction("b", 200)))
```

We will then `coalesce` our data to one partition. `coalesce()` is a very important aspect. If we want to save our data in a single file, we need to `coalesce` it into one, but there is an important implication of doing so:

```
rdd.coalesce(1).saveAsTextFile(FileName)
```

If we `coalesce` it to a single file, then only one executor can save the data to our system. This means that saving the data will be very slow and, also, there will be a risk of being out of memory because all data will be sent to one executor. Generally, in the production environment, we save it as many partitions, based on the executors available, or even multiplied by its own factor. So, if we have 16 executors, then we can save it to 64. But this results in 64 files. For test purposes, we will save it to one file, as shown in the preceding code snippet:

```
rdd.coalesce (numPartitions = 1).saveAsTextFile(FileName)
```

Now, we'll load the data. We only need to pass the filename to the `TextFile` method and it will return `fromFile`:

```
val fromFile = spark.textFile(FileName)
```

We then assert our data, which will yield `theSameElementsAS List`, `UserTransaction(a,100)`, and `UserTransaction(b,200)`:

```
fromFile.collect().toList should contain theSameElementsAs List(
    "UserTransaction(a,100)", "UserTransaction(b,200)"
    //note - this is string!
  )
 }
}
```

The important thing to note is that for a list of strings, Spark doesn't know the schema of our data because we are saving it in plain text.

This is one of the points to note when it comes to saving plain text, because loading the data is not easy, since we need to manually map every string to `UserTransaction`. So, we will have to parse every record manually, but, for test purposes, we will treat our transaction as strings.

Now, let's start the test and see the structure of the folder that was created:

In the preceding screenshot, we can see that our test passed and that we get
`transactions.txt`. Inside the folder, we have four files. The first one is `._SUCCESS.crc`,
which means that the save succeeded. Next, we have `.part-00000.crc`, to control and
validate that everything worked properly, which means that the save was proper. We then
have `_SUCCESS` and `part-00000`, where both files have checksum, but `part-00000` has all
the data as well. Then, we also have `UserTransaction(a,100)` and
`UserTransaction(b,200)`:

In the next section, we will learn what will happen if we increment the number of
partitions.

Leveraging JSON as a data format

In this section, we will leverage JSON as a data format and save our data in JSON. The following topics will be covered:

- Saving data in JSON format
- Loading JSON data
- Testing

This data is human-readable and gives us more meaning than simple plain text because it carries some schema information, such as a field name. We will then learn how to save data in JSON format and load our JSON data.

We will first create a DataFrame of `UserTransaction("a", 100)` and `UserTransaction("b", 200)`, and use `.toDF()` to save the DataFrame API:

```
val rdd = spark.sparkContext
        .makeRDD(List(UserTransaction("a", 100), UserTransaction("b",
200)))
        .toDF()
```

We will then issue `coalesce()` and, this time, we will take the value as 2, and we will have two resulting files. We will then issue the `write.format` method and, for the same, we need to specify a format, for which we will use the `json` format:

```
rdd.coalesce(2).write.format("json").save(FileName)
```

If we use the unsupported format, we will get an exception. Let's test this by entering the source as `not`:

```
rdd.coalesce(2).write.format("not").save(FileName)
```

We will get exceptions such as `'This format is not expected'`, `'Failed to find data source: not'`, and `'There is no such data source'`:

```
Run:    SaveJSON
      ✓ ⊘      Tests failed: 1 of 1 test
   ▼  Test Res
      ▼  Save  Failed to find data source: not. Please find packages at http://spark-packages.org
             java.lang.ClassNotFoundException: Failed to find data source: not. Please find packages at
             http://spark-packages.org
                 at org.apache.spark.sql.execution.datasources.DataSource.lookupDataSource(DataSource.scala:145)
                 at org.apache.spark.sql.execution.datasources.DataSource.providingClass$lzycompute(DataSource
             .scala:78)
                 at org.apache.spark.sql.execution.datasources.DataSource.providingClass(DataSource.scala:78)
                 at org.apache.spark.sql.execution.datasources.DataSource.write(DataSource.scala:427)
                 at org.apache.spark.sql.DataFrameWriter.save(DataFrameWriter.scala:211)
                 at org.apache.spark.sql.DataFrameWriter.save(DataFrameWriter.scala:194)
                 at com.tomekl007.chapter_4.SaveJSON$$anonfun$1.apply$mcV$sp(SaveJSON.scala:26)
                 at com.tomekl007.chapter_4.SaveJSON$$anonfun$1.apply(SaveJSON.scala:18)
                 at com.tomekl007.chapter_4.SaveJSON$$anonfun$1.apply(SaveJSON.scala:18)
                 at org.scalatest.Transformer$$anonfun$apply$1.apply$mcV$sp(Transformer.scala:22)
                 at org.scalatest.OutcomeOf$class.outcomeOf(OutcomeOf.scala:85)
                 at org.scalatest.OutcomeOf$.outcomeOf(OutcomeOf.scala:104)
```

In our original JSON code, we will specify the format and we need to save it to `FileName`. If we want to read, we need to specify it as `read` mode and also add a path to the folder:

```
val fromFile = spark.read.json(FileName)
```

On this occasion, let's comment out `afterEach()` to investigate the produced JSON:

```
// override def afterEach() {
// val path = Path(FileName)
// path.deleteRecursively()
// }
```

Let's start the test:

```
fromFile.show()
assert(fromFile.count() == 2)
}
}
```

The output is as follows:

```
+------+------+
|amount|userId|
|   200|     b|
|   100|     a|
+------+------+
```

In the preceding code output, we can see that our test passed and that the DataFrame includes all the meaningful data.

From the output, we can see that DataFrame has all the schema required. It has `amount` and `userId`, which is very useful.

The `transactions.json` folder has two parts—one part is `r-00000`, and the other part is `r-00001`, because we issued two partitions. If we save the data in a production system with 100 partitions, we will end up with 100 part files and, furthermore, every part file will have a CRC checksum file.

This is the first file:

```
{"userId":"a","amount":"100"}
```

Here, we have a JSON file with schema and, hence, we have a `userID` field and `amount` field.

On the other hand, we have the second file with the second record with `userID` and `amount` as well:

```
{"userId":"b","amount":"200"}
```

The advantage of this is that Spark is able to infer the data from the schema and is loaded in a formatted DataFrame with proper naming and types. The disadvantage, however, is that every record has some additional overhead. Every record needs to have a string in it and, in each string, if we have a file that has millions of files and we are not compressing it, there will be substantial overhead, which is not ideal.

JSON is human-readable but, on the other hand, it consumes a lot of resources, just like the CPU for compressing, reading, and writing, and also the disk and memory for the overhead. Apart from JSON, there are better formats that we will cover in the following sections.

In the next section, we will look at the tabular format, where we will cover a CSV file that is often used to import to Microsoft Excel or Google spreadsheet. This is also a very useful format for data scientists, but only while using smaller datasets.

Tabular formats – CSV

In this section, we will be covering text data, but in a tabular format—CSV. The following topics will be covered:

- Saving data in CSV format
- Loading CSV data
- Testing

Saving CSV files is even more involved than JSON and plain text because we need to specify whether we want to retain headers of our data in our CSV file.

First, we will create a DataFrame:

```
test("should save and load CSV with header") {
 //given
 import spark.sqlContext.implicits._
 val rdd = spark.sparkContext
 .makeRDD(List(UserTransaction("a", 100), UserTransaction("b", 200)))
 .toDF()
```

Then, we will use the `write` format CSV. We also need to specify that we don't want to include the `header` option in it:

```
//when
rdd.coalesce(1)
    .write
    .format("csv")
    .option("header", "false")
    .save(FileName)
```

We will then perform a test to verify whether the condition is `true` or `false`:

```
//when
rdd.coalesce(1)
   .write
   .format("csv")
   .option("header", "true")
   .save(FileName)
```

Also, we don't need to add any additional dependency to support CSV, as required in the previous versions.

We will then specify the `read` mode, which should be similar to the `write` mode, and we need to specify whether we have a `header` or not:

```
val fromFile = spark.read.option("header", "false").csv(FileName)
```

Let's start the test and check the output:

```
+---+---+
|_c0|_c1|
+---+---+
|  a|100|
|  b|200|
+---+---+
```

In the preceding code output, we can see that the data is loaded, but we lost our schema. c0 and c1 are the aliases for column 0 (c0) and column 1 (c1) that were created by Spark.

So, if we are specifying that the `header` should retain that information, let's specify the `header` at the `write` and also at the `read`:

```
val fromFile = spark.read.option("header", "true").csv(FileName)
```

We will specify that the `header` should retain our information. In the following output, we can see that the information regarding the schema was perceived throughout the read and write operation:

```
+------+------+
|userId|amount|
+------+------+
|     a|   100|
|     b|   200|
+------+------+
```

Let's see what happens if we `write` with the `header` and `read` without it. Our test should fail, as demonstrated in the following code screenshot:

In the preceding screenshot, we can see that our test failed because we don't have a schema as we were reading without headers. The first record, which was a `header`, was treated as the column value.

Let's try a different situation, where we are writing without `header` and reading with `header`:

```
    //when
  rdd.coalesce(1)
      .write
      .format("csv")
      .option("header", "false")
      .save(FileName)

  val fromFile = spark.read.option("header", "false").csv(FileName)
```

Our test will fail again because this time, we treated our first record as the header record.

Let's set both the read and write operations with `header` and test our code after removing the comment we added previously:

```
override def afterEach() {
    val path = Path(FileName)
    path.deleteRecursively()
}
```

The CSV and JSON files will have schema, but with less overhead. Therefore, it could be even better than JSON.

In the next section, we'll see how we can use a schema-based format as a whole with Spark.

Using Avro with Spark

So far, we have looked at text-based files. We worked with plain text, JSON, and CSV. JSON and CSV are better than plain text because they carry some schema information.

In this section, we'll be looking at an advanced schema, known as Avro. The following topics will be covered:

- Saving data in Avro format
- Loading Avro data
- Testing

Avro has a schema and data embedded within it. This is a binary format and is not human-readable. We will learn how to save data in Avro format, load it, and then test it.

First, we will create our user transaction:

```
test("should save and load avro") {
//given
import spark.sqlContext.implicits._
val rdd = spark.sparkContext
    .makeRDD(List(UserTransaction("a", 100), UserTransaction("b", 200)))
    .toDF()
```

We will then do a `coalesce` and write an Avro:

```
//when
rdd.coalesce(2)
    .write
    .avro(FileName)
```

While using CSV, we specified the format like CSV, and, when we specified JSON, this, too, was a format. But in Avro, we have a method. This method is not a standard Spark method; it is from a third-party library. To have Avro support, we need to access `build.sbt` and add `spark-avro` support from `com.databricks`.

We then need to import the proper method. We will import `com.databricks.spark.avro._` to give us the implicit function that is extending the Spark DataFrame:

```
import com.databricks.spark.avro._
```

We are actually using an Avro method and we can see that `implicit class` takes a `DataFrameWriter` class, and writes our data in Spark format.

In the `coalesce` code we used previously, we can use `write`, specify the format, and execute a `com.databricks.spark.avro` class. `avro` is a shortcut to not write `com.databricks.spark.avro` as a whole string:

```
//when
  rdd.coalesce(2)
      .write.format(com.databricks.spark.avro)
      .avro(FileName)
```

In short, there is no need to specify the format; just apply the implicit `avro` method.

Let's comment out the code and remove Avro to check how it saves:

```
// override def afterEach() {
   // val path = Path(FileName)
   // path.deleteRecursively()
// }
```

If we open the `transactions.avro` folder, we have two parts—`part-r-00000` and `part-r-00001`.

The first part will have binary data. It consists of a number of binary records and some human-readable data, which is our schema:

We have two fields—`user ID`, which is a type string or null, and `name: amount`, which is an integer. Being a primitive type, JVM cannot have null values. The important thing to note is that, in production systems, we have to save really large datasets, and there will be thousands of records. The schema is always in the first line of every file. If we check the second part as well, we will see that there is exactly the same schema and then the binary data.

Usually, we have only one or more lines if you have a complex schema, but still, it is a very low amount of data.

We can see that in the resulting dataset, we have `userID` and `amount`:

```
+------+------+
|userId|amount|
+------+------+
|     a|   100|
|     b|   200|
+------+------+
```

In the preceding code block, we can see that the schema was portrayed in the file. Although it is a binary file, we can extract it.

In the next section, we will be looking at the columnar format—Parquet.

Columnar formats – Parquet

In this section, we'll be looking at the second schema-based format, Parquet. The following topics will be covered:

- Saving data in Parquet format
- Loading Parquet data
- Testing

This is a columnar format, as the data is stored column-wise and not row-wise, as we saw in the JSON, CSV, plain text, and Avro files.

This is a very interesting and important format for big data processing and for making the process faster. In this section, we will focus on adding Parquet support to Spark, saving the data into the filesystem, reloading it again, and then testing. Parquet is similar to Avro as it gives you a `parquet` method but this time, it is a slightly different implementation.

In the `build.sbt` file, for the Avro format, we need to add an external dependency, but for Parquet, we already have that dependency within Spark. So, Parquet is the way to go for Spark because it is inside the standard package.

Let's have a look at the logic that's used in the `SaveParquet.scala` file for saving and loading Parquet files.

First, we coalesce the two partitions, specify the format, and then specify that we want to save `parquet`:

```
package com.tomekl007.chapter_4

import com.databricks.spark.avro._
import com.tomekl007.UserTransaction
import org.apache.spark.sql.SparkSession
import org.scalatest.{BeforeAndAfterEach, FunSuite}

import scala.reflect.io.Path

class SaveParquet extends FunSuite with BeforeAndAfterEach {
  val spark = SparkSession.builder().master("local[2]").getOrCreate()

  private val FileName = "transactions.parquet"

  override def afterEach() {
    val path = Path(FileName)
    path.deleteRecursively()
  }
```

```
test("should save and load parquet") {
  //given         '
  import spark.sqlContext.implicits._
  val rdd = spark.sparkContext
    .makeRDD(List(UserTransaction("a", 100), UserTransaction("b", 200)))
    .toDF()

  //when
  rdd.coalesce(2)
    .write
    .parquet(FileName)
```

The `read` method also implements exactly the same method:

```
val fromFile = spark.read.parquet(FileName)

fromFile.show()
assert(fromFile.count() == 2)
  }


}
```

Let's begin this test but, before that, we will comment out the following code withing our `SaveParquet.scala` file to see the structure of the files:

```
//    override def afterEach() {
//    val path = Path(FileName)
//    path.deleteRecursively()
//  }
```

A new `transactions.parquet` folder gets created and we have two parts inside it—`part-r-00000` and `part-r-00001`. This time, however, the format is entirely binary and there is some metadata embedded with it.

We have the metadata embedded and also the `amount` and `userID` fields, which are of the `string` type. The part `r-00000` is exactly the same and has the schema embedded. Hence, Parquet is also a schema-based format. When we read the data, we can see that we have the `userID` and `amount` columns available.

Summary

In this chapter, we learned how to save data in plain text format. We noticed that schema information is lost when we do not load the data properly. We then learned how to leverage JSON as a data format and saw that JSON retains the schema, but it has a lot of overhead because the schema is for every record. We then learned about CSV and saw that Spark has embedded support for it. The disadvantage of this approach, however, is that the schema is not about the specific types of records, and tabs need to be inferred implicitly. Toward the end of this chapter, we covered Avro and Parquet, which have columnar formats that are also embedded with Spark.

In the next chapter, we'll be working with Spark's key/value API.

11
Working with the Spark Key/Value API

In this chapter, we'll be working with the Spark key/value API. We will start by looking at the available transformations on key/value pairs. We will then learn how to use the `aggregateByKey` method instead of the `groupBy()` method. Later, we'll be looking at actions on key/value pairs and looking at the available partitioners on key/value data. At the end of this chapter, we'll be implementing an advanced partitioner that will be able to partition our data by range.

In this chapter, we will be covering the following topics:

- Available actions on key/value pairs
- Using aggregateByKey instead of groupBy()
- Actions on key/value pairs
- Available partitioners on key/value data
- Implementing a custom partitioner

Available actions on key/value pairs

In this section, we will be covering the following topics:

- Available transformations on key/value pairs
- Using `countByKey()`
- Understanding the other methods

So, this is our well-known test in which we will be using transformations on key/value pairs.

First, we will create an array of user transactions for users A, B, A, B, and C for some amount, as per the following example:

```
val keysWithValuesList =
Array(
UserTransaction("A", 100),
UserTransaction("B", 4),
UserTransaction("A", 100001),
UserTransaction("B", 10),
UserTransaction("C", 10)
)
```

We then need to key our data by a specific field, as per the following example:

```
val keyed = data.keyBy(_.userId)
```

We will key it by userId, by invoking the keyBy method with a userId parameter.

Now, our data is assigned to the keyed variable and its type is a tuple. The first element is a string, that is, userId and the second element is UserTransaction.

Let's look at the transformations that are available. First, we will look at countByKey.

Let's look at its implementation, as shown in the following example:

```
val data = spark.parallelize(keysWithValuesList)
 val keyed = data.keyBy(_.userId)
//when
 val counted = keyed.countByKey()
// keyed.combineByKey()
// keyed.aggregateByKey()
// keyed.foldByKey()
// keyed.groupByKey()
//then
 counted should contain theSameElementsAs Map("B" -> 2, "A" -> 2, "C" -> 1)
```

This returns a Map of key K, and Long is a generic type because it can be any type of key. In this example, the key will be a string. Every operation that returns map is not entirely safe. If you see a signature of the method that is returning map, it is a sign that this data will be sent to the driver and it needs to fit in the memory. If there is too much data to fit into one driver's memory, then we will run out of memory. Hence, we need to be cautious when using this method.

We then perform an assert count that should contain the same elements as the map, as per the following example:

```
counted should contain theSameElementsAs Map("B" -> 2, "A" -> 2, "C" -> 1)
```

`B` is 2 because we have two values for it. Also, `A` is one similar to `C` as they have only one value. `CountByKey()` is not memory expensive because it only stores key and counter. However, if the key is a complex and a big object, for example, a transaction with multiple fields, which is more than two, then that map could be really big.

But let's start this test, as shown in the following example:

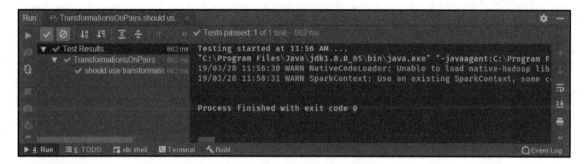

From the preceding screenshot, we can see that our test passed.

We also have a `combineByKey()` method, which combines the same elements for the same key, and shares the negative `aggregateByKey()` that is able to aggregate different types. We have `foldByKey`, which is taking the current state and value, but returns the same type as the value for the key.

We also have `groupByKey()`, which we learned about in the previous section. This groups everything by the specific key and returns the iterator of values for a key. This is a very memory expensive operation as well, so we need to be careful when we use it.

In the next section, we'll be using `aggregateByKey` instead of `groupBy`. We will learn how `groupBy` works and fix its shortcomings.

Using aggregateByKey instead of groupBy()

In this section, we will explore the reason why we use `aggregateByKey` instead of `groupBy`.

We will cover the following topics:

- Why we should avoid the use of `groupByKey`
- What `aggregateByKey` gives us
- Implementing logic using `aggregateByKey`

First, we will create our array of user transactions, as shown in the following example:

```
val keysWithValuesList =
Array(
UserTransaction("A", 100),
UserTransaction("B", 4),
UserTransaction("A", 100001),
UserTransaction("B", 10),
UserTransaction("C", 10)
)
```

We will then use `parallelize` to create an RDD, as we want our data to be key-wise. This is shown in the following example:

```
val data = spark.parallelize(keysWithValuesList)
val keyed = data.keyBy(_.userId)
```

In the preceding code, we invoked `keyBy` for `userId` to have the data of payers, key, and user transaction.

Let's consider that we want to aggregate, where we want to execute some specific logic for the same key, as shown in the following example:

```
val aggregatedTransactionsForUserId = keyed
.aggregateByKey(amountForUser)(addAmount, mergeAmounts)
```

The reasoning for this can be for choosing a maximum element, minimum element, or to calculate average. `aggregateByKey` needs to take three parameters, as shown in the following example:

```
aggregateByKey(amountForUser)(addAmount, mergeAmounts)
```

The first parameter is an initial parameter of type T, and defining `amountForUser` is an initial parameter that has a type of `ArrayBuffer`. This is very important because the Scala compiler will infer that type, and argument numbers 1 and 2 need to have exactly the same type T in this example: `ArrayBuffer.empty[long]`.

The next argument is a method that takes the current element that we are processing. In this example, `transaction: UserTransaction) =>` is a current transaction and also needs to take the state that we were initializing our function with, and, hence, it will be an array buffer here.

It needs to be of the same type that's as shown in the following code block, so this is our type T:

```
mutable.ArrayBuffer.empty[Long]
```

At this point, we are able to take any transaction and add it to the specific state. This is done in a distributed way. For one key, execution is done on one executor and, for exactly the same key, on different executors. This happens in parallel, so multiple trades will be added for the same key.

Now, Spark knows that, for exactly the same key, it has multiple states of type T `ArrayBuffer` that it needs to merge. So, we need to `mergeAmounts` for our transactions for the same key.

The `mergeArgument` is a method that takes two states, both of which are intermediate states of type T, as shown in the following code block:

```
val mergeAmounts = (p1: mutable.ArrayBuffer[Long], p2:
mutable.ArrayBuffer[Long]) => p1 ++= p2
```

In this example, we want to merge the release buffers into one array buffer. Therefore, we issue `p1 ++= p2`. This will merge two array buffers into one.

Now, we have all arguments ready and we are able to execute `aggregateByKey` and see what the results look like. The result is an RDD of string and type T, the `ArrayBuffer[long]`, which is our state. We will not be keeping `UserTransaction` in our RDD anymore, which helps in reducing the amount of memory. `UserTransaction` is a heavy object because it can have multiple fields and, in this example, we are only interested in the amount field. So, this way, we can reduce the memory that is used.

The following example shows what our result should look like:

```
aggregatedTransactionsForUserId.collect().toList should contain
theSameElementsAs List(
  ("A", ArrayBuffer(100, 100001)),
  ("B", ArrayBuffer(4,10)),
  ("C", ArrayBuffer(10)))
```

We should have a key, A, and an `ArrayBuffer` of `100` and `10001`, since it is our input data. B should be `4` and `10`, and lastly, C should be `10`.

Let's start the test to check if we have implemented `aggregateByKey` properly, as shown in the following example:

From the preceding output, we can see that it worked as expected.

In the next section, we'll be looking at the actions that are available on key/value pairs.

Actions on key/value pairs

In this section, we'll be looking at the actions on key/value pairs.

We will cover the following topics:

- Examining actions on key/value pairs
- Using `collect()`
- Examining the output for the key/value RDD

In the first section of this chapter, we covered transformations that are available on key/value pairs. We saw that they are a bit different compared to RDDs. Also, for actions, it is slightly different in terms of result but not in the method name.

Therefore, we'll be using `collect()` and we'll be examining the output of our action on these key/value pairs.

First, we will create our transactions array and RDD according to `userId`, as shown in the following example:

```
val keysWithValuesList =
Array(
UserTransaction("A", 100),
UserTransaction("B", 4),
UserTransaction("A", 100001),
UserTransaction("B", 10),
UserTransaction("C", 10)
)
```

The first action that comes to our mind is to `collect()`. `collect()` takes every element and assigns it to the result, and thus our result is very different than the result of `keyBy`.

Our result is a pair of keys, `userId`, and a value, that is, `UserTransaction`. We can see, from the following example, that we can have a duplicated key:

```
res should contain theSameElementsAs List(
("A",UserTransaction("A",100)),
("B",UserTransaction("B",4)),
("A",UserTransaction("A",100001)),
("B",UserTransaction("B",10)),
("C",UserTransaction("C",10))
)//note duplicated key
```

As we can see in the preceding code, we have multiple occurrences of the same order. For a simple key as a string, duplication is not very expensive. However, if we have a more complex key, it will be expensive.

So, let's start this test, as shown in the following example:

We can see, from the preceding output, that our test has passed. To see the other actions, we will look at different methods.

If a method is returning RDD, such as `collect[U] (f: PartialFunction[(String, UserTransaction), U])`, it means that this is not an action. If something returns RDD, it means that it is not an action. This is the case for key/value pairs.

`collect()` does not return an RDD but returns an array, thus it is an action. `count` returns `long`, so this is also an action. `countByKey` returns map. If we want to `reduce` our elements, then this is an action, but `reduceByKey` is not an action. This is the big difference between `reduce` and `reduceByKey`.

We can see that everything is normal according to the RDD, so actions are the same and differences are only in transformation.

In the next section, we will be looking at the available partitioners on key/value data.

Available partitioners on key/value data

We know that partitioning and partitioners are the key components of Apache Spark. They influence how our data is partitioned, which means they influence where the data actually resides on which executors. If we have a good partitioner, then we will have good data locality, which will reduce shuffle. We know that shuffle is not desirable for processing, so reducing shuffle is crucial, and, therefore, choosing a proper partitioner is also crucial for our systems.

In this section, we will cover the following topics:

- Examining `HashPartitioner`
- Examining `RangePartitioner`
- Testing

We will first examine our `HashPartitioner` and `RangePartitioner`. We will then compare them and test the code using both the partitioners.

First we will create a `UserTransaction` array, as per the following example:

```
val keysWithValuesList =
Array(
UserTransaction("A", 100),
UserTransaction("B", 4),
UserTransaction("A", 100001),
UserTransaction("B", 10),
UserTransaction("C", 10)
)
```

We will then use `keyBy` (as shown in the following example) because the partitioner will automatically work on the key for our data:

```
val keyed = data.keyBy(_.userId)
```

We will then take a `partitioner` of key data, as shown in the following example:

```
val partitioner = keyed.partitioner
```

The code shows `partitioner.isEmpty`, because we have not defined any `partitioner` and thus it is empty at this point, as can be seen in the following example:

```
assert(partitioner.isEmpty)
```

We can specify a `partitioner` by using the `partitionBy` method, as shown in the following example:

```
val hashPartitioner = keyed.partitionBy(new HashPartitioner(100))
```

The method is expecting a `partitioner` abstract class implementation. We will have a couple of implementations, but first, let's focus on `HashPartitioner`.

`HashPartitioner` takes a number of partitions and has a number of partitions. `numPartition` returns our argument, but `getPartition` gets a bit more involved, as shown in the following example:

```
def numPartitions: Int = partitions
def getPartition(key: Any): int = key match {
    case null => 0
    case_ => Utils.nonNegativeMode(key.hashCode, numPartitions)
}
```

It first checks if our `key` is `null`. If it is `null`, it will land in partition number 0. If we have data with `null` keys, they will all land in the same executors, and, as we know, this is not a good situation because the executors will have a lot of memory overhead and they can fail without memory exceptions.

If the `key` is not `null`, then it does a `nonNegativeMod` from `hashCode` and the number of partitions. It has to be the modulus of the number of partitions so that it can be assigned to the proper partition. Thus, the `hashCode` method is very important for our key.

If we are supplying a custom key and not a primitive type like an integer or string, which has a well-known `hashCode`, we need to supply and implement a proper `hashCode` as well. But the best practice is to use the `case` class from Scala as they have `hashCode` and equals implemented for you.

We have defined `partitioner` now, but `partitioner` is something that could be changed dynamically. We can change our `partitioner` to be `rangePartitioner`. `rangePartitioner` takes the partitions in an RDD.

`rangePartitioner` is more complex as it tries to divide our data into ranges, which is not as simple as `HashPartitioner` is in getting partition. The method is really complex as it is trying to spread our data evenly and has complex logic for spreading that into ranges.

Let's start our test to check if we were able to assign `partitioner` properly, as shown in the following output:

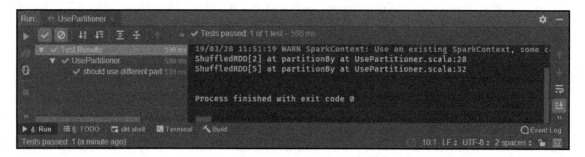

Our tests have passed. This means that, at the initial point, the `partitioner` was empty and then we had to shuffle RDD at `partitionBy`, and also a `branchPartitioner`. But it shows us only the number line where we created an instance of the `partitioner` interface.

In the next section, we'll try to improve it or try to tweak and play with the partitioner by implementing a custom partitioner.

Implementing a custom partitioner

In this section, we'll implement a custom partitioner and create a partitioner that takes a list of parses with ranges. If our key falls into a specific range, we will assign the partition number index of the list.

We will cover the following topics:

- Implementing a custom partitioner
- Implementing a range partitioner
- Testing our partitioner

We will implement the logic range partitioning based on our own range partitioning and then test our partitioner. Let's start with the black box test without looking at the implementation.

The first part of the code is similar to what we have used already, but this time we have `keyBy` amount of data, as shown in the following example:

```
val keysWithValuesList =
Array(
UserTransaction("A", 100),
UserTransaction("B", 4),
UserTransaction("A", 100001),
UserTransaction("B", 10),
UserTransaction("C", 10)
)
val data = spark.parallelize(keysWithValuesList)
val keyed = data.keyBy(_.amount)
```

We are keying by the amount and we have the following keys: 100, 4, 100001, 10, and 10.

We will then create a partitioner and call it `CustomRangePartitioner`, which will take a list of tuples, as shown in the following example:

```
val partitioned = keyed.partitionBy(new
CustomRangePartitioner(List((0,100), (100, 10000), (10000, 1000000))))
```

The first element is from 0 to 100, which means if the key is within the range of 0 to 100, it should go to partition 0. So, we have four keys that should fall into that partition. The next partition number has a range of 100 and 10000, so every record within that range should fall into partition number 1, inclusive of both ends. The last range is between 10000 and 1000000 elements, so, if the record is between that range, it should fall into that partition. If we have an element out of range, then the partitioner will fail with an illegal argument exception.

Let's look at the following example, which shows the implementation of our custom range partitioner:

```
class CustomRangePartitioner(ranges: List[(Int,Int)]) extends Partitioner{
  override def numPartitions: Int = ranges.size
override def getPartition(key: Any): Int = {
 if(!key.isInstanceOf[Int]){
 throw new IllegalArgumentException("partitioner works only for Int type")
 }
 val keyInt = key.asInstanceOf[Int]
 val index = ranges.lastIndexWhere(v => keyInt >= v._1 && keyInt <= v._2)
 println(s"for key: $key return $index")
 index
 }
 }
```

It takes ranges as an argument list of tuples, as shown in the following example:

```
(ranges: List[(Int,Int)])
```

Our `numPartitions` should be equal to `ranges.size`, so the number of partitions is equal to the number of ranges in size.

Next, we have the `getPartition` method. First, our partitioner will work only for integers, as shown in the following example:

```
if(!key.isInstanceOf[Int])
```

We can see that this is an integer and cannot be used for other types. For the same reason, we first need to check whether our key is an instance of integer, and, if it is not, we get an `IllegalArgumentException` because that partitioner works only for the int type.

We can now test our `keyInt` by using `asInstanceOf`. Once this is done, we are able to iterate over ranges and take the last range when the index is between predicates. Our predicate is a tuple v, and should be as follows:

```
val index = ranges.lastIndexWhere(v => keyInt >= v._1 && keyInt <= v._2)
```

KeyInt should be more than or equal to `v._1`, which is the first element of the tuple, but it should also be lower than the second element, `v._2`.

The start of the range is `v._1` and the end of the range is `v._2`, so we can check that our element is within range.

In the end, we will print the for key we found in the index for debugging purposes, and we will return the index, which will be our partition. This is shown in the following example:

```
println(s"for key: $key return $index")
```

Let's start the following test:

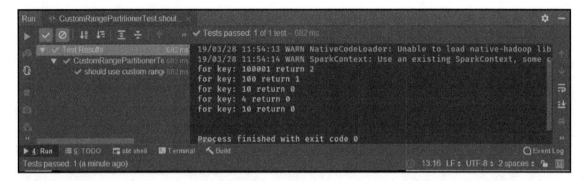

We can see that for key `100001`, the code returned partition number 2, which is as expected. For key `100` returns partition one and for `10`, `4`, `10` it returns partition zero, which means our code works as expected.

Summary

In this chapter, we first saw available the transformations on key/value pairs. We then learned how to use `aggregateByKey` instead of `groupBy`. We also covered actions on key/value pairs. Later, we looked at available partitioners like `rangePartitioner` and `HashPartition` on key/value data. By the end of this chapter, we had implemented our custom partitioner, which was able to assign partitions, based on the end and start of the range for learning purposes.

In the next chapter, we will learn how to test our Spark jobs and Apache Spark jobs.

12
Testing Apache Spark Jobs

In this chapter, we will test Apache Spark jobs and learn how to separate logic from the Spark engine.

We will first cover unit testing of our code, which will then be used by the integration test in SparkSession. Later, we will be mocking data sources using partial functions, and then learn how to leverage ScalaCheck for property-based testing for a test as well as types in Scala. By the end of this chapter, we will have performed tests in different versions of Spark.

In this chapter, we will be covering the following topics:

- Separating logic from Spark engine-unit testing
- Integration testing using SparkSession
- Mocking data sources using partial functions
- Using ScalaCheck for property-based testing
- Testing in different versions of Spark

Separating logic from Spark engine-unit testing

Let's start by separating logic from the Spark engine.

In this section, we will cover the following topics:

- Creating a component with logic
- Unit testing of that component
- Using the case class from the model class for our domain logic

Let's look at the logic first and then the simple test.

So, we have a `BonusVerifier` object that has only one method, `quaifyForBonus`, that takes our `userTransaction` model class. According to our login in the following code, we load user transactions and filter all users that are qualified for a bonus. First, we need to test it to create an RDD and filter it. We need to create a SparkSession and also create data for mocking an RDD or DataFrame, and then test the whole Spark API. Since this involves logic, we will test it in isolation. The logic is as follows:

```
package com.tomekl007.chapter_6
import com.tomekl007.UserTransaction
object BonusVerifier {
 private val superUsers = List("A", "X", "100-million")
 def qualifyForBonus(userTransaction: UserTransaction): Boolean = {
  superUsers.contains(userTransaction.userId) && userTransaction.amount >
100
  }
}
```

We have a list of super users with the `A`, `X`, and `100-million` user IDs. If our `userTransaction.userId` is within the `superUsers` list, and if the `userTransaction.amount` is higher than `100`, then the user qualifies for a bonus; otherwise, they don't. In the real world, the qualifier for bonus logic will be even more complex, and thus it is very important to test the logic in isolation.

The following code shows our test using the `userTransaction` model. We know that our user transaction includes `userId` and `amount`. The following example shows our domain model object, which is shared between a Spark execution integration test and our unit testing, separated from Spark:

```
package com.tomekl007

import java.util.UUID

case class UserData(userId: String , data: String)

case class UserTransaction(userId: String, amount: Int)

case class InputRecord(uuid: String = UUID.randomUUID().toString(), userId:
String)
```

We need to create our `UserTransaction` for user ID X and the amount `101`, as shown in the following example:

```scala
package com.tomekl007.chapter_6
import com.tomekl007.UserTransaction
import org.scalatest.FunSuite
class SeparatingLogic extends FunSuite {
test("test complex logic separately from spark engine") {
 //given
 val userTransaction = UserTransaction("X", 101)
//when
 val res = BonusVerifier.qualifyForBonus(userTransaction)
//then
 assert(res)
 }
}
```

We will then pass `userTransaction` to `qualifyForBonus` and the result should be `true`. This user should qualify for a bonus, as shown in the following output:

Now, let's write a test for the negative use case, as follows:

```scala
test(testName = "test complex logic separately from spark engine - non
qualify") {
 //given
 val userTransaction = UserTransaction("X", 99)
//when
 val res = BonusVerifier.qualifyForBonus(userTransaction)
//then
 assert(!res)
 }
```

Here, we have a user, X, that spends 99 for which our results should be false. When we validate our code, we can see, from the following output, that our test has passed:

We have covered two cases, but in real-world scenarios, there are many more. For example, if we want to test the case where we are specifying userId, which is not from this superuser list, and we have some_new_user that spends a lot of money, in our case, 100000, we get the following result:

```
test(testName = "test complex logic separately from spark engine - non
qualify2") {
 //given
 val userTransaction = UserTransaction("some_new_user", 100000)
//when
 val res = BonusVerifier.qualifyForBonus(userTransaction)
//then
 assert(!res)
 }
```

Let's assume that it should not qualify, and so such logic is a bit complex. Therefore, we are testing it in a unit test way:

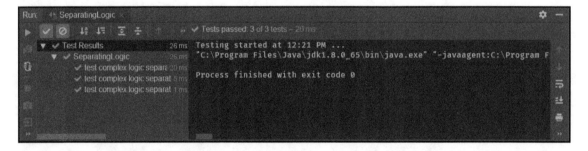

Our tests are very fast and so we are able to check that everything works as expected without introducing Spark at all. In the next section, we'll be changing the logic with integration testing using SparkSession.

Integration testing using SparkSession

Let's now learn about integration testing using SparkSession.

In this section, we will cover the following topics:

- Leveraging SparkSession for integration testing
- Using a unit tested component

Here, we are creating the Spark engine. The following line is crucial for the integration test:

```
val spark: SparkContext =
SparkSession.builder().master("local[2]").getOrCreate().sparkContext
```

It is not a simple line just to create a lightweight object. SparkSession is a really heavy object and constructing it from scratch is an expensive operation from the perspective of resources and time. Tests such as creating SparkSession will take more time compared to the unit testing from the previous section.

For the same reason, we should use unit tests often to convert all edge cases and use integration testing only for the smaller part of the logic, such as the capital edge case.

The following example shows the array we are creating:

```
val keysWithValuesList =
Array(
UserTransaction("A", 100),
UserTransaction("B", 4),
UserTransaction("A", 100001),
UserTransaction("B", 10),
UserTransaction("C", 10)
)
```

The following example shows the RDD we are creating:

```
val data = spark.parallelize(keysWithValuesList)
```

This is the first time that Spark has been involved in our integration testing. Creating an RDD is also a time-consuming operation. Compared to just creating an array, it is really slow to create an RDD because that is also a heavy object.

We will now use our `data.filter` to pass a `qualifyForBonus` function, as shown in the following example:

```
val aggregatedTransactionsForUserId =
data.filter(BonusVerifier.qualifyForBonus)
```

This function was already unit tested, so we don't need to consider all edge cases, different IDs, different amounts, and so on. We are just creating a couple of IDs with some amounts to test whether or not our whole chain of logic is working as expected.

After we have applied this logic, our output should be similar to the following:

```
UserTransaction("A", 100001)
```

Let's start this test and check how long it takes to execute a single integration test, as shown in the following output:

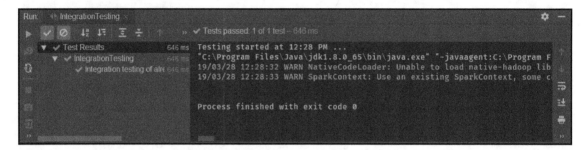

It took around `646 ms` to execute this simple test.

If we want to cover every edge case, the value will be multiplied by a factor of hundreds compared to the unit test from the previous section. Let's start this unit test with three edge cases, as shown in the following output:

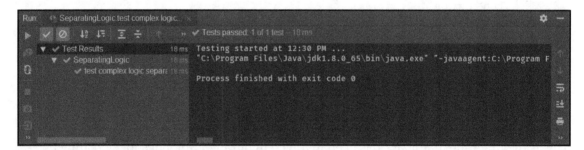

We can see that our test took only `18 ms`, which means that it was 20 times faster, even though we covered three edge cases, compared to integration tests with only one case.

Here, we have covered a lot of logic with hundreds of edge cases, and we can conclude that it is really wise to have unit tests at the lowest possible level.

In the next section, we will be mocking data sources using partial functions.

Mocking data sources using partial functions

In this section, we will cover the following topics:

- Creating a Spark component that reads data from Hive
- Mocking the component
- Testing the mock component

Let's assume that the following code is our production line:

```
ignore("loading data on prod from hive") {
UserDataLogic.loadAndGetAmount(spark, HiveDataLoader.loadUserTransactions)
}
```

Here, we are using the `UserDataLogic.loadAndGetAmount` function, which needs to load our user data transaction and get the amount of the transaction. This method takes two arguments. The first argument is a `sparkSession` and the second argument is the `provider` of `sparkSession`, which takes `SparkSession` and returns `DataFrame`, as shown in the following example:

```
object UserDataLogic {
  def loadAndGetAmount(sparkSession: SparkSession, provider: SparkSession
=> DataFrame): DataFrame = {
    val df = provider(sparkSession)
    df.select(df("amount"))
  }
}
```

For production, we will load user transactions and see that the `HiveDataLoader` component has only one method, `sparkSession.sql`, and (`"select * from transactions"`), as shown in the following code block:

```
object HiveDataLoader {
  def loadUserTransactions(sparkSession: SparkSession): DataFrame = {
  sparkSession.sql("select * from transactions")
  }
}
```

This means that the function goes to Hive to retrieve our data and returns a DataFrame. According to our logic, it executes the `provider` that is returning a DataFrame and from a DataFrame, it is only selecting `amount`.

This logic is not simple we can test because our SparkSession `provider` is interacting with the external system in production. So, we can create a function such as the following:

```
UserDataLogic.loadAndGetAmount(spark, HiveDataLoader.loadUserTransactions)
```

Let's see how to test such a component. First, we will create a DataFrame of user transactions, which is our mock data, as shown in the following example:

```
val df = spark.sparkContext
.makeRDD(List(UserTransaction("a", 100), UserTransaction("b", 200)))
.toDF()
```

However, we need to save the data to Hive, embed it, and then start Hive.

Since we are using the partial functions, we can pass a partial function as a second argument, as shown in the following example:

```
val res = UserDataLogic.loadAndGetAmount(spark, _ => df)
```

The first argument is `spark`, but it is not used in our method this time. The second argument is a method that is taking SparkSession and returning DataFrame.

However, our execution engine, architecture, and code do not consider whether this SparkSession is used or if the external call is made; it only wants to return DataFrame. We can _ our first argument because it's ignored and just return DataFrame as the return type.

And so our `loadAndGetAmount` will get a mock DataFrame, which is the DataFrame that we created.

But, for the logic shown, it is transparent and doesn't consider whether the DataFrame comes from Hive, SQL, Cassandra, or any other source, as shown in the following example:

```
val df = provider(sparkSession)
df.select(df("amount"))
```

In our example, `df` comes from the memory that we created for the purposes of the test. Our logic continues and it selects the amount.

Then, we show our columns, `res.show()`, and that logic should end up with one column amount. Let's start this test, as shown in the following example:

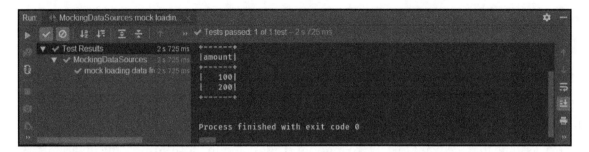

We can see from the preceding example that our resulting DataFrame has one column amount in `100` and `200` values. This means it worked as expected, without the need to start an embedding Hive. The key here is to use a provider and not embed our select start within our logic.

In the next section, we'll be using ScalaCheck for property-based tests.

Using ScalaCheck for property-based testing

In this section, we will cover the following topics:

- Property-based testing
- Creating a property-based test

Let's look at a simple property-based test. We need to import a dependency before we define properties. We also need a dependency for the ScalaCheck library, which is a library for property-based tests.

In the previous section, every test extended `FunSuite`. We used functional tests, but we had to provide arguments explicitly. In this example, we're extending `Properties` from the ScalaCheck library and testing a `StringType`, as follows:

```
object PropertyBasedTesting extends Properties("StringType")
```

Our ScalaCheck will generate a random string for us. If we create a property-based test for a custom type, then that is not known to the ScalaCheck. We need to provide a generator that will generate instances of that specific type.

First, let's define the first property of our string type in the following way:

```
property("length of strings") = forAll { (a: String, b: String) =>
  a.length + b.length >= a.length
}
```

`forAll` is a method from the ScalaCheck property. We will pass an arbitrary number of arguments here, but they need to be of the type that we are testing.

Let's assume that we want to get two random strings, and in those strings, the invariants should be perceived.

If we are adding the length of string `a` to the length of string `b`, the sum of that should be greater or equal to `a.length`, because if `b` is `0` then it will be equal, as shown in the following example:

```
a.length + b.length >= a.length
```

However, this is an invariant of `string` and for every input string, it should be `true`.

The second property that we are defining is a bit more complex, as shown in the following code:

```
property("creating list of strings") = forAll { (a: String, b: String, c:
String) =>
  List(a,b,c).map(_.length).sum == a.length + b.length + c.length
}
```

In the preceding code, we asked the ScalaCheck runtime engine to share three strings this time, that is, `a`, `b`, and `c`. We will test this when we create a list of strings.

Here, we are creating a list of strings, that is, `a`, `b`, `c`, as shown in the following code:

```
List(a,b,c)
```

When we map every element to `length`, the sum of those elements should be equal to adding everything by length. Here, we have `a.length + b.length + c.length` and we will test the collections API to check if the map and other functions work as expected.

Let's start this property-based test to check if our properties are correct, as shown in the following example:

We can see that the `StringType.length` property of `string` passed and executed `100` tests. It could be surprising that `100` tests were executed, but let's try to see what was passed as the arguments by using the following code:

```
println(s"a: $a, b: $b")
```

We will print the `a` argument and `b` argument, and retry our property by testing the following output:

We can see that a lot of weird strings were generated, so this is an edge case that we were not able to create up-front. Property-based testing will create a very weird unique code that isn't a proper string. So, this is a great tool for testing whether our logic is working as expected for a specific type.

In the next section, we'll be testing in different versions of Spark.

Testing in different versions of Spark

In this section, we will cover the following topics:

- Changing the component to work with Spark pre-2.x
- Mock testing pre-2.x
- RDD mock testing

Let's start with the mocking data sources from the third section of this chapter—*Mocking data sources using partial functions.*

Since we were testing `UserDataLogic.loadAndGetAmount,` notice that everything operates on the DataFrame and thus we had a SparkSession and DataFrame.

Now, let's compare it to the Spark pre-2.x. We can see that this time, we are unable to use DataFrames. Let's assume that the following example shows our logic from the previous Sparks:

```
test("mock loading data from hive"){
 //given
 import spark.sqlContext.implicits._
 val df = spark.sparkContext
 .makeRDD(List(UserTransaction("a", 100), UserTransaction("b", 200)))
 .toDF()
 .rdd
//when
 val res = UserDataLogicPre2.loadAndGetAmount(spark, _ => df)
//then
 println(res.collect().toList)
 }
}
```

We can see that we are not able to use DataFrames this time.

In the previous section, `loadAndGetAmount` was taking `spark` and DataFrame, but the DataFrame in the following example is an RDD, not a DataFrame anymore, and so we are passing an `rdd`:

```
val res = UserDataLogicPre2.loadAndGetAmount(spark, _ => rdd)
```

However, we need to create a different `UserDataLogicPre2` for Spark that takes SparkSession and returns an RDD after mapping an RDD of an integer, as shown in the following example:

```
object UserDataLogicPre2 {
 def loadAndGetAmount(sparkSession: SparkSession, provider: SparkSession =>
RDD[Row]): RDD[Int] = {
 provider(sparkSession).map(_.getAs[Int]("amount"))
 }
}
object HiveDataLoaderPre2 {
 def loadUserTransactions(sparkSession: SparkSession): RDD[Row] = {
 sparkSession.sql("select * from transactions").rdd
 }
}
```

In the preceding code, we can see that the `provider` is executing our provider logic, mapping every element, getting it as an `int`. Then, we get the amount. `Row` is a generic type that can have a variable number of arguments.

> In Spark pre-2.x, we do not have `SparkSession` and therefore we need to use `SparkContext` and change our login accordingly.

Summary

In this chapter, we first learned how to separate logic from the Spark engine. We then looked at a component that was well-tested in separation without the Spark engine, and we carried out integration testing using SparkSession. For this, we created a SparkSession test by reusing the component that was already well-tested. By doing that, we did not have to cover all edge cases in the integration test and our test was much faster. We then learned how to leverage partial functions to supply mocked data that's provided at the testing phase. We also covered ScalaCheck for property-based testing. By the end of this chapter, we had tested our code in different versions of Spark and learned how to change our DataFrame mock test to RDD.

In the next chapter, we will learn how to leverage the Spark GraphX API.

13
Leveraging the Spark GraphX API

In this chapter, we will learn how to create a graph from a data source. We will then carry out experiments with the Edge API and Vertex API. By the end of this chapter, you will know how to calculate the degree of vertex and PageRank.

In this chapter, we will cover the following topics:

- Creating a graph from a data source
- Using the Vertex API
- Using the Edge API
- Calculating the degree of vertex
- Calculating PageRank

Creating a graph from a data source

We will be creating a loader component that will be used to load the data, revisit the graph format, and load a Spark graph from file.

Creating the loader component

The `graph.g` file consists of a structure of vertex to vertex. In the following `graph.g` file, if we align 1 to 2, this means that there is an edge between vertex ID 1 and vertex ID 2. The second line means that there's an edge from vertex ID 1 to 3, then from 2 to 3, and finally 3 to 5:

```
1   2
1   3
2   3
3   5
```

We will take the `graph.g` file, load it, and see how it will provide results in Spark. First, we need to get a resource to our `graph.g` file. We will do this using the `getClass.getResource()` method to get the path to it, as follows:

```
package com.tomekl007.chapter_7

import org.apache.spark.SparkContext
import org.apache.spark.sql.SparkSession
import org.scalatest.FunSuite

class CreatingGraph extends FunSuite {
  val spark: SparkContext =
SparkSession.builder().master("local[2]").getOrCreate().sparkContext

  test("should load graph from a file") {
    //given
    val path = getClass.getResource("/graph.g").getPath
```

Revisiting the graph format

Next, we have the `GraphBuilder` method, which is our own component:

```
    //when
    val graph = GraphBuilder.loadFromFile(spark, path)
```

The following is our `GraphBuilder.scala` file for our `GraphBuilder` method:

```
package com.tomekl007.chapter_7

import org.apache.spark.SparkContext
import org.apache.spark.graphx.{Graph, GraphLoader}

object GraphBuilder {

  def loadFromFile(sc: SparkContext, path: String): Graph[Int, Int] = {
    GraphLoader.edgeListFile(sc, path)
  }
}
```

It uses a `GraphLoader` class from the `org.apache.spark.graphx.{Graph, GraphLoader}` package and we are specifying the format.

The format that's specified here is `edgeListFile`. We are passing the `sc` parameter, which is the `SparkContext` and `path` parameter, which contains the path of where the file is placed. The resulting graph will be `Graph [Int, Int]`, which we will use as the identifier of our vertices.

Loading Spark from file

Once we have the resulting graph, we can pass the `spark` and `path` parameters to our `GraphBuilder.loadFromFile()` method, and at this point, we'll have a `graph` that is a construct graph of `Graph [Int, Int]`, as follows:

```
val graph = GraphBuilder.loadFromFile(spark, path)
```

To iterate and validate that our graph was properly loaded, we will use `triplets` from `graph`, which are a pair of vertex to vertex and also an edge between those vertices. We will see that the structure of the graph was loaded properly:

```
//then
graph.triplets.foreach(println(_))
```

At the end, we are asserting that we get 4 triplets (as shown earlier in the *Creating the loader component* section, we have four definitions from the `graph.g` file):

```
        assert(graph.triplets.count() == 4)
    }


}
```

We will start the test and see whether we are able to load our graph properly.

We get the following output. Here, we have (2, 1), (3, 1), (3,1), (5,1), (1,1), (2,1), (1,1), and (3,1):

Hence, according to the output graph, we were able to reload our graph using Spark.

Using the Vertex API

In this section, we will construct the graph using edge. We will learn to use the Vertex API and also leverage edge transformations.

Constructing a graph using the vertex

Constructing a graph is not a trivial task; we need to supply vertices and edges between them. Let's focus on the first part. The first part consists of our `users`, `users` is an RDD of `VertexId` and `String` as follows:

```
package com.tomekl007.chapter_7

import org.apache.spark.SparkContext
import org.apache.spark.graphx.{Edge, Graph, VertexId}
import org.apache.spark.rdd.RDD
```

```
import org.apache.spark.sql.SparkSession
import org.scalatest.FunSuite

class VertexAPI extends FunSuite {
  val spark: SparkContext =
SparkSession.builder().master("local[2]").getOrCreate().sparkContext

  test("Should use Vertex API") {
    //given
    val users: RDD[(VertexId, (String))] =
      spark.parallelize(Array(
        (1L, "a"),
        (2L, "b"),
        (3L, "c"),
        (4L, "d")
      ))
```

VertexId is of the long type; this is only a type alias for Long:

```
type VertexID = Long
```

But since our graph sometimes has a lot of content, the VertexId should be unique and a very long number. Every vertex in our vertices' RDD should have a unique VertexId. The custom data associated with the vertex can be any class, but we will go for simplicity with the String class. First, we are creating a vertex with ID 1 and string data a, the next with ID 2 and string data b, the next with ID 3 and string data c, and similarly for the data with ID 4 and string d, as follows:

```
val users: RDD[(VertexId, (String))] =
  spark.parallelize(Array(
    (1L, "a"),
    (2L, "b"),
    (3L, "c"),
    (4L, "d")
  ))
```

 Creating a graph from only vertices will be correct but not very useful. A graph is the best way to find relationships between the data, which is why a graph is the main building block for social networks.

Creating couple relationships

In this section, we will create couple relationships and edges between our vertices. Here, we'll have a relationship that is an `Edge`. An `Edge` is a case class from the `org.apache.spark.graphx` package. It is a bit more involved because we need to specify the source vertex ID and destination vertex ID. We want to specify that vertex ID 1 and 2 have a relationship, so let's make a label for this relationship. In the following code, we will specify vertex ID 1 and ID 2 as a `friend`, then we will specify vertex ID 1 and ID 3 as a `friend` as well. Lastly, vertex ID 2 and ID 4 will be a `wife`:

```
val relationships =
  spark.parallelize(Array(
    Edge(1L, 2L, "friend"),
    Edge(1L, 3L, "friend"),
    Edge(2L, 4L, "wife")
  ))
```

Also, a label could be of any type—it doesn't need to be a `String` type; we can type what we want and pass it. Once we have our vertices, users, and edge relationships, we can create a graph. We are using the `Graph` class' `apply` method to construct our Spark GraphX graph. We need to pass `users`, `VertexId`, and `relationships`, as follows:

Returning `graph` is an RDD, but it's a special RDD:

```
val graph = Graph(users, relationships)
```

When we go to the `Graph` class, we will see that the `Graph` class has an RDD of `vertices` and an RDD of `edges`, so the `Graph` class is a companion object for two RDDs, as shown in the following screenshot:

```scala
*/
val vertices: VertexRDD[VD]

/**
 * An RDD containing the edges and their associated attributes.  The entries in the RDD contain
 * just the source id and target id along with the edge data.
 *
 * @return an RDD containing the edges in this graph
 *
 * @see [[Edge]] for the edge type.
 * @see [[Graph#triplets]] to get an RDD which contains all the edges
 * along with their vertex data.
 *
 */
val edges: EdgeRDD[ED]

/**
 * An RDD containing the edge triplets, which are edges along with the vertex data associated with
 * the adjacent vertices. The caller should use [[edges]] if the vertex data are not needed, i.e.
 * if only the edge data and adjacent vertex ids are needed.
 *
 * @return an RDD containing edge triplets
 *
 * @example This operation might be used to evaluate a graph
 * coloring where we would like to check that both vertices are a
 * different color.
 * {{{
 * type Color = Int
 * val graph: Graph[Color, Int] = GraphLoader.edgeListFile("hdfs://file.tsv")
 * val numInvalid = graph.triplets.map(e => if (e.src.data == e.dst.data) 1 else 0).sum
 * }}}
 */
```

We can get the underlying RDD of `vertices` and `edges` by issuing some methods. For example, if you want to get all the vertices, we can map all vertices and we will get the attribute and `VertexId`. Here, we are only interested in the attribute and we will convert it into uppercase, as follows:

```scala
val res = graph.mapVertices((_, att) => att.toUpperCase())
```

The following are the attributes:

```scala
val users: RDD[(VertexId, (String))] =
  spark.parallelize(Array(
    (1L, "a"),
    (2L, "b"),
    (3L, "c"),
    (4L, "d")
  ))
```

Once we convert it into uppercase, we can just collect all the vertices and perform `toList()`, as follows:

```
        println(res.vertices.collect().toList)
    }


  }
```

We can see that after applying the transformation to the values, our graph has the following vertices:

Using the Edge API

In this section, we will construct the graph using the Edge API. We'll also use the vertex, but this time we'll focus on the edge transformations.

Constructing the graph using edge

As we saw in the previous sections, we have edges and vertices, which is an RDD. As this is an RDD, we can get an edge. We have a lot of methods that are available on the normal RDD. We can use the `max` method, `min` method, `sum` method, and all other actions. We will apply the `reduce` method, so the `reduce` method will take two edges, we will take `e1`, `e2`, and we can perform some logic on it.

The `e1` edge is an edge that has an attribute, destination, and a source, as shown in the following screenshot:

```
val resFromFilter = graph.edges.filter((e1) => e1.
println(resFromFilter)                              attr                              String
                                                    dstId                   graphx.VertexId
val res = graph.mapEdges(e => e.attr.toUpperC       srcId                   graphx.VertexId
                                                    otherVertexId(vid: graphx.VertexI… graphx.VertexId
println(res.edges.collect().toList)                 relativeDirection(vid: graphx.Verte… EdgeDirection
                                                    copy[ED](srcId: graphx.VertexId = Edge.t… Edge[ED]
geAPI   λ(e1: Any)                                  clone()                          AnyRef
e Vertex API ×                                      hashCode()                          Int
ed: 1 of 1 test – 1 s 2 ms                          toString()                       String
```

Since the edge is chaining together two vertices, we can perform some logic here. For example, if the `e1` edge attribute is equal to `friend`, we want to lift an edge using the `filter` operation. So, the `filter` method is taking only one edge, and then if the edge `e1` is a `friend`, it will be perceived automatically. We can see that at the end we can `collect` it and perform a `toList` so that the API that is on Spark is available for our use. The following code will help us implement our logic:

```
import org.apache.spark.SparkContext
import org.apache.spark.graphx.{Edge, Graph, VertexId}
import org.apache.spark.rdd.RDD
import org.apache.spark.sql.SparkSession
import org.scalatest.FunSuite

class EdgeAPI extends FunSuite {
  val spark: SparkContext =
SparkSession.builder().master("local[2]").getOrCreate().sparkContext

  test("Should use Edge API") {
    //given
    val users: RDD[(VertexId, (String))] =
      spark.parallelize(Array(
        (1L, "a"),
        (2L, "b"),
        (3L, "c"),
        (4L, "d")
      ))

    val relationships =
      spark.parallelize(Array(
        Edge(1L, 2L, "friend"),
        Edge(1L, 3L, "friend"),
        Edge(2L, 4L, "wife")
      ))
```

```
val graph = Graph(users, relationships)

//when
val resFromFilter = graph.edges.filter((e1) => e1.attr ==
"friend").collect().toList
println(resFromFilter)
```

It also has a couple of methods on the top of the standard RDD. For example, we can do a map edge, which will take an edge, and we can take an attribute and map every label to uppercase, as follows:

```
val res = graph.mapEdges(e => e.attr.toUpperCase)
```

 On the graph, we can also perform group edges. Grouping edges is similar to GROUP BY, but only for edges.

Type the following command to print line-mapping edges:

```
println(res.edges.collect().toList)
```

Let's start our code. We can see in the output that our code has filtered the wife edge—we only perceive the friend edge from vertex ID 1 to ID 2, and also vertex ID 1 to ID 3, and map edges as shown in the following screenshot:

```
Run:    EdgeAPI.Should use Edge API
        Tests passed: 1 of 1 test – 885 ms
885 ms   Testing started at 2:51 PM ...
885 ms   "C:\Program Files\Java\jdk1.8.0_65\bin\java.exe" "-javaagent:C:\Program Files\JetBrains\IntelliJ II
885 ms   19/03/28 14:51:19 WARN NativeCodeLoader: Unable to load native-hadoop library for your platform..
         19/03/28 14:51:20 WARN SparkContext: Use an existing SparkContext, some configuration may not take
         [Stage 0:>                                                    (0 + 0) / 2]19/03/28 14:51:21
         [rdd_12_0]
         19/03/28 14:51:21 WARN Executor: 1 block locks were not released by TID = 1:
         [rdd_12_1]
         List(Edge(1,2,friend), Edge(1,3,friend))
         19/03/28 14:51:21 WARN Executor: 1 block locks were not released by TID = 2:
         [rdd_12_0]
         19/03/28 14:51:21 WARN Executor: 1 block locks were not released by TID = 3:
         [rdd_12_1]
         List(Edge(1,2,FRIEND), Edge(1,3,FRIEND), Edge(2,4,WIFE))

         Process finished with exit code 0

4: Run    6: TODO    sbt shell    Terminal    Build                              Event Log
```

Calculating the degree of the vertex

In this section, we will cover the total degree, then we'll split it into two parts—an in-degree and an out-degree—and we will understand how this works in the code.

For our first test, let's construct the graph that we already know about:

```
package com.tomekl007.chapter_7

import org.apache.spark.SparkContext
import org.apache.spark.graphx.{Edge, Graph, VertexId}
import org.apache.spark.rdd.RDD
import org.apache.spark.sql.SparkSession
import org.scalatest.FunSuite
import org.scalatest.Matchers._

class CalculateDegreeTest extends FunSuite {
  val spark: SparkContext =
SparkSession.builder().master("local[2]").getOrCreate().sparkContext

  test("should calculate degree of vertices") {
    //given
    val users: RDD[(VertexId, (String))] =
      spark.parallelize(Array(
        (1L, "a"),
        (2L, "b"),
        (3L, "c"),
        (4L, "d")
      ))


    val relationships =
      spark.parallelize(Array(
        Edge(1L, 2L, "friend"),
        Edge(1L, 3L, "friend"),
        Edge(2L, 4L, "wife")
      ))
```

We can get the degrees using the `degrees` method. The `degrees` method is returning `VertexRDD` because `degrees` is a vertex:

```
val graph = Graph(users, relationships)

//when
val degrees = graph.degrees.collect().toList
```

The result is as follows:

```
//then
degrees should contain theSameElementsAs List(
    (4L,  1L),
    (2L,  2L),
    (1L,  2L),
    (3L,  1L)
  )
}
```

The preceding code explains that for the `4L` instance of `VertexId`, there is only one relationship because there is a relationship between `2L` and `4L`.

Then, for the `2L` instance of `VertexId`, there are two, so it is between `1L`, `2L` and `2L`, `4L`. For the `1L` instance of `VertexId`, there are two, which are `1L`, `2L` and `1L`, `3L`, and for `VertexId` `3L`, there is only one relationship, between `1L` and `3L`. This way, we can check how our graph is coupled and how many relationships there are. We can find out which vertex is best known by sorting them, so we can see that our test passed in the following screenshot:

The in-degree

The in-degree tells us how many vertices come into the second vertex, but not the other way around. This time, we can see that for the `2L` instance of `VertexId`, there's only one inbound vertex. We can see that `2L` has a relationship with `1L`, `3L` has a relationship with `1L` as well, and `4L` has a relationship with `1L`. In the following resulting dataset, there will be no data for `VertexId` `1L`, because `1L` is the input. So, `1L` would only be a source and not a destination:

```
test("should calculate in-degree of vertices") {
    //given
    val users: RDD[(VertexId, (String))] =
```

```
  spark.parallelize(Array(
    (1L, "a"),
    (2L, "b"),
    (3L, "c"),
    (4L, "d")
  ))


val relationships =
  spark.parallelize(Array(
    Edge(1L, 2L, "friend"),
    Edge(1L, 3L, "friend"),
    Edge(2L, 4L, "wife")
  ))

val graph = Graph(users, relationships)

//when
val degrees = graph.inDegrees.collect().toList

//then
degrees should contain theSameElementsAs List(
  (2L, 1L),
  (3L, 1L),
  (4L, 1L)
)
}
```

The preceding characteristic of the in-degree is a very useful property. We use the in-degree
when we are unable to find out which of our pages are very important because they are
linked through the page, not from it.

By running this test, we can see that it works as expected:

The out-degree

The out-degree explains how many vertices are going out. This time, we'll be calculating the sources of our edges, relationships, and not destinations, like we did in the in-degree method.

To get the out-degree, we will use the following code:

```
val degrees = graph.outDegrees.collect().toList
```

The `outDegrees` method contains both `RDD` and `VertexRDD`, which we have collected to a list using the `collect` and `toList` methods.

Here, `VertexId 1L` should have two outbound vertices because there is a relationship between `1L`, `2L` and `1L`, `3L`:

```
test("should calculate out-degree of vertices") {
  //given
  val users: RDD[(VertexId, (String))] =
    spark.parallelize(Array(
      (1L, "a"),
      (2L, "b"),
      (3L, "c"),
      (4L, "d")
    ))


  val relationships =
    spark.parallelize(Array(
      Edge(1L, 2L, "friend"),
      Edge(1L, 3L, "friend"),
      Edge(2L, 4L, "wife")
    ))

  val graph = Graph(users, relationships)

  //when
  val degrees = graph.outDegrees.collect().toList

  //then
  degrees should contain theSameElementsAs List(
    (1L, 2L),
    (2L, 1L)
  )
}

}
```

Also, `VertexId 2L` should have one outbound vertex as there is a relationship between `2L` and `4L` and not the other way around, as shown in the preceding code.

We will run this test and get the following output:

Calculating PageRank

In this section, we will load data about users and reload data about their followers. We will use the graph API and the structure of our data, and we will calculate PageRank to calculate the rank of users.

First, we need to load `edgeListFile`, as follows:

```
package com.tomekl007.chapter_7

import org.apache.spark.graphx.GraphLoader
import org.apache.spark.sql.SparkSession
import org.scalatest.FunSuite
import org.scalatest.Matchers._

class PageRankTest extends FunSuite {
  private val sc =
SparkSession.builder().master("local[2]").getOrCreate().sparkContext

  test("should calculate page rank using GraphX API") {
    //given
    val graph = GraphLoader.edgeListFile(sc,
getClass.getResource("/pagerank/followers.txt").getPath)
```

170

We have a `followers.txt` file; the following screenshot shows the format of the file, which is similar to the file we saw in the *Creating the loader component* section:

We can see that there's a relationship between each of the vertex IDs. Hence, we are loading the `graph` from the `followers.txt` file and then issuing PageRank. We are taking `vertices` that will be needed, as follows:

```
val ranks = graph.pageRank(0.0001).vertices
```

PageRank will calculate the influence and relationship between our vertices.

Loading and reloading data about users and followers

To find out which user has which name, we need to load the `users.txt` file. The `users.txt` file assigns the `VertexId` with a username and its own name. We use the following code:

```
val users =
sc.textFile(getClass.getResource("/pagerank/users.txt").getPath).map { line
=>
```

The following is the `users.txt` file:

```
1,BarackObama,Barack Obama
2,ladygaga,Goddess of Love
3,jeresig,John Resig
4,justinbieber,Justin Bieber
6,matei_zaharia,Matei Zaharia
7,odersky,Martin Odersky
8,anonsys
```

We are splitting on the comma and the first group is our integer, which will be vertex ID, and then `fields(1)` is the name of vertex, as follows:

```
val fields = line.split(",")
(fields(0).toLong, fields(1))
}
```

Next, we will `join` the `users` with `ranks`. We will `join` the `users` using the `VertexId` by using the `username` and `rank` of the user. Once we have that, we can sort everything by the `rank`, so we will take a second element of the tuple and it should be sorted as `sortBy` `((t) =>t.2`. At the beginning of the file, we will have the user with the most influence:

```
//when
val rankByUsername = users.join(ranks).map {
    case (_, (username, rank)) => (username, rank)
}.sortBy((t) => t._2, ascending = false)
    .collect()
    .toList
```

We will print the following and order the `rankByUsername`, as follows:

```
println(rankByUsername)
//then
rankByUsername.map(_._1) should contain theSameElementsInOrderAs List(
    "BarackObama",
    "ladygaga",
    "odersky",
    "jeresig",
    "matei_zaharia",
    "justinbieber"
  )
}

}
```

If we skip the `sortBy` method, Spark does not guarantee any ordering of elements; to keep the ordering, we need to issue the `sortBy` method.

After running the code, we get the following output:

```
Run    PageRankTest should calculate pa...
    ✓  ✓ Tests passed: 1 of 1 test – 7 s 423 ms
7 s 423 ms  [rdd_896_0]
   7 s 423 ms  List((BarackObama,1.4588814096664682), (ladygaga,1.390049198216498), (odersky,1.2973176314422592)
   7 s 423 ms  , (jeresig,0.9993442038507723), (matei_zaharia,0.7013599933629602), (justinbieber,0.15))

            Process finished with exit code 0
```

When we start running this test, we can see whether the GraphX PageRank was able to calculate the influence of our users. We get the output that's shown in the preceding screenshot, where BarackObama was first with 1.45 influence, then ladygaga with an influence of 1.39, odersky with 1.29, jeresig with 0.99, matai_zaharia with 0.70, and at the end, justinbieber with an influence of 0.15.

From the preceding information, we were able to calculate complex algorithms with a minimal amount of code.

Summary

In this chapter, we delved into transformations and actions, and then we learned about Spark's immutable design. We studied how to avoid shuffle and how to reduce operational expenses. Then, we looked at how to save the data in the correct format. We also learned how to work with the Spark key/value API, and how to test Apache Spark jobs. After that, we learned how to create a graph from a data source, and then we investigated and experimented with the edge and vertex APIs. We learned how to calculate the degree of the vertex. Finally, we looked at PageRank and how we are able to calculate it using the Spark GraphicX API.

Other Books You May Enjoy

If you enjoyed this book, you may be interested in these other books by Packt:

Learning PySpark
Tomasz Drabas, Denny Lee

ISBN: 978-1-78646-370-8

- Learn about Apache Spark and the Spark 2.0 architecture
- Build and interact with Spark DataFrames using Spark SQL
- Learn how to solve graph and deep learning problems using GraphFrames and TensorFrames respectively
- Read, transform, and understand data and use it to train machine learning models
- Build machine learning models with MLlib and ML
- Learn how to submit your applications programmatically using spark-submit
- Deploy locally built applications to a cluster

PySpark Cookbook
Tomasz Drabas, Denny Lee

ISBN: 978-1-78883-536-7

- Configure a local instance of PySpark in a virtual environment
- Install and configure Jupyter in local and multi-node environments
- Create DataFrames from JSON and a dictionary using pyspark.sql
- Explore regression and clustering models available in the ML module
- Use DataFrames to transform data used for modeling
- Connect to PubNub and perform aggregations on streams

Leave a review - let other readers know what you think

Please share your thoughts on this book with others by leaving a review on the site that you bought it from. If you purchased the book from Amazon, please leave us an honest review on this book's Amazon page. This is vital so that other potential readers can see and use your unbiased opinion to make purchasing decisions, we can understand what our customers think about our products, and our authors can see your feedback on the title that they have worked with Packt to create. It will only take a few minutes of your time, but is valuable to other potential customers, our authors, and Packt. Thank you!

Index

F

faster average computations
  with aggregate 43, 44
file
  Spark, loading from 147
filter function 26

G

Gnu on Windows (GOW)
  download link 10
graph format 146, 147
graph
  constructing, edges used 152, 153, 154
  constructing, vertex used 148
  creating, from data source 145
GraphX (graph) 8

H

hypotheses
  testing, on large datasets 53, 54

I

immutability
  in highly concurrent environment 82, 83, 84
integration testing
  with SparkSession 135, 136

J

join 90, 91
JSON
  leveraging, as data format 106, 107, 108

K

key-value paired data points
  pivot tabling 45, 46
key/value data
  partitioners 124, 126
key/value pairs
  actions 117, 118, 122, 124
keyBy() operations
  used, for reducing shuffle 94, 95, 96

L

loader component
  creating 146
logic
  separating, from Spark engine-unit testing 131, 132, 133, 134

M

map function
  about 26
  averages, calculating with 41, 42
MapReduce function 9
MLlib
  about 8, 10, 49
  summary statistics, computing with 50, 51

P

PageRank
  calculating 159, 160
  rank of users, calculating 160, 162
parallelization
  about 22
  with Spark RDDs 22, 23, 24, 25
parent
  RDD, chaining with 76, 77
Parquet data
  loading 115
Parquet format
  data, saving in 114
partial functions
  used, for mocking data sources 137, 138
partitioners
  on key/value data 124, 126
Pearson correlation
  about 51
  versus Spearman correlation 52
pivot tabling
  with key-value paired data points 45, 46
plain text format
  data, saving in 102, 103, 104, 105
process
  shuffle, detecting in 87, 88, 89
property-based testing
  ScalaCheck, using for 139, 140, 141